ROUND ABOUT TH

Round About
the Little Steeple

THE STORY OF
A WILTSHIRE PARSON
1573–1623

BY

IDA GANDY

ALAN SUTTON 1989
Published in collaboration with

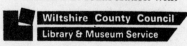
Wiltshire County Council
Library & Museum Service

ALAN SUTTON PUBLISHING
BRUNSWICK ROAD · GLOUCESTER

First published in 1960 by
George Allen & Unwin Limited, London.

This edition published in 1989

British Library Cataloguing in Publication Data

Gandy, Ida
   Round about the Little Steeple.
   1. Wiltshire. Social life, history
   I. Title
   942.3′1

ISBN 0–86299–593–0

Cover picture: The Bridgeman Art Gallery.

Printed and bound in Great Britain by
The Guernsey Press Co. Ltd, Guernsey, Channel Islands.

Mr. Ferraby, the Minister of Bishops Cannings, was an ingenious man and an excellent musician. . . . The parish in those days would have challenged all England for music, football, and ringing.

JOHN AUBREY

Bishops Cannnings Church, Wilts
S.E. View

PREFACE

As children we looked across our vicarage field at a beautiful church with a tall spire and a little steeple. The sound of the bells, which we learned to ring ourselves, was constantly in our ears.

During our wanderings on the surrounding downs we sometimes passed a few small shaggy trees that stood just where an old coaching road crossed a famous dyke. Here, we were told, a predecessor of my father's had called on Queen Anne, wife of James I, to stop and listen to the bells, and had entertained her with music and singing by his parishioners.

This book attempts to reconstruct a much-loved village both at that period, and—more briefly—today, together with an account of the Queen's visit and of a later one by the King.

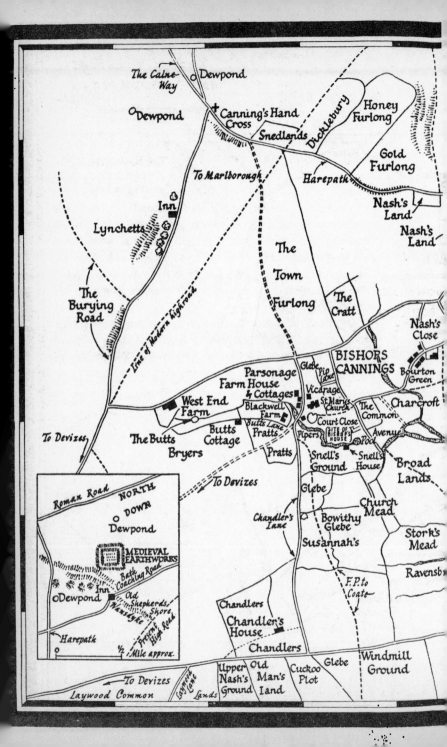

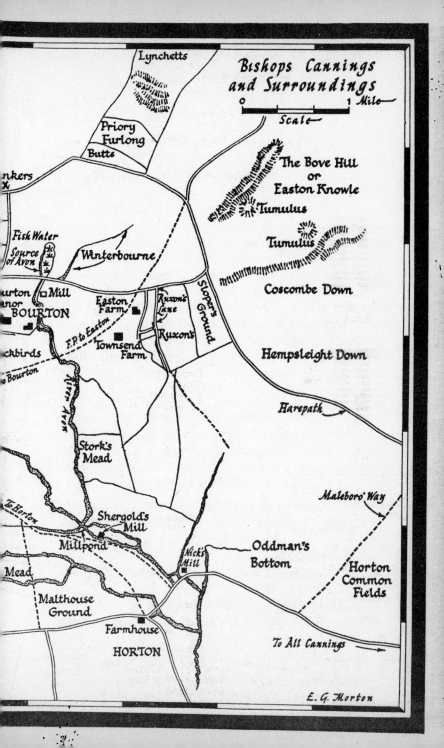

ACKNOWLEDGEMENTS

Many people have helped me to write this book. I am grateful to them all, but more especially to Richard Sandell, Hon. Librarian of the Wilts Archaeological Society's library at Devizes Museum; to certain old Cannings friends; to Esther Reid for her map and Susan Williams-Ellis, who designed the jacket. I am also indebted to Maurice Rathbone and Irvine Gray, County Archivists for Wilts. and Glos.; to the Crown Commissioners for letting me examine the seventeenth century Court Books in their possession; to the Bodleian Library for permission to search for, and reproduce, George Ferrebe's 'Shepherds' Song' from the Aubrey M.S.S.; to the Librarian of Magdalen College, Oxford; to the Diocesan Registrar; and to Penguin Publications for a verse by William Strode, from their *Anthology of English Verse*.

ABBREVIATIONS USED IN THE NOTES

V.C.H. VII. Victoria County History of Wilts. Vol. VII.

W.A.M. Wilts. Archaeological Magazine.

Q.S.G.R. ed. B. H. Cunnington. Quarter Session Great Rolls for the Seventeenth Century ed. B. H. Cunnington.

OTHER IMPORTANT SOURCES

J. Aubrey, *The Natural History of Wiltshire* in *The Topographical Collections of John Aubrey*, ed. J. E. Jackson (Devizes 1862).

Sir Thomas Phillipps, *Institutiones Clericorum in Comitatu Wiltoniae* (1825).

[J. Waylen], *History of Devizes* (1859).

Court Books for the Manor of Bourton (property of the Crown Commissioners).

CONTENTS

Biographical Introduction

Ida Gandy (née Hony) was born in 1885. Her paternal ancestors had been for generations parsons or landowners, often both, first in Cornwall and later in Wiltshire. Her grandfather was a fellow of Exeter College, Oxford, held one of the college livings and later became Archdeacon of Sarum, living partly in the close at Salisbury. He was an enthusiastic botanist, geologist and archaeologist. His son, Ida's father, was vicar of Bishops Cannings near Devizes and later of neighbouring Woodborough. Her mother's family were engineers, builders and timber merchants; Ida's maternal grandfather, Stephen Lewin, was a keen student of church architecture. When only twenty-one he published a book illustrated by himself on Lincolnshire churches; later he submitted a design for the Albert Memorial and designed and made railway engines. Emphatically not the typical parson's wife of the 1880s, his daughter could not sew a button on straight or sing a hymn in tune; she allowed the children to run barefoot and put the girls into serge knickers instead of the then correct white frilly drawers. She frequently entered literary competitions in the newspapers and once won a prize with a review of a play she had never seen.

Her daughter Ida was always a compulsive writer. Another of her enthusiasms was for social reform. After a short semi-academic stay in Oxford with a University family, she set off to undertake social work in London – again, not the conventional choice for a young girl of good family. A job with the Workers' Educational Association took her to Peppard in south Oxfordshire where she met the local GP, Dr Thomas Gandy, whom she married in 1915. He became Chairman of the local Labour Party – even less 'the thing' in those days.

Dr Gandy and his wife stayed in Peppard for fifteen years and had three children. Mrs Gandy began to write and stage plays for the local amateurs, some of which were published and widely performed. She also wrote children's books; her *Three Bold Explorers*, based on the childhood experiences of herself and her siblings, was followed in 1929 by *Sunset Island*, in which legendary supernatural figures – Kelpies, Boggarts, Leprechauns (she had read them all up in the British Museum) – were pictured as surviving together on a distant western island. Then in 1930 came her first well-known book, *A Wiltshire Childhood* (reprinted in 1988 by Alan Sutton Publishing). J.C. Squire published one of her short stories in the *London Mercury*, then the leading literary periodical.

Ida had for years pined for wilder country than the already urbanized landscape of south Oxfordshire and in 1930 she persuaded her husband to move to Clunbury in Shropshire, the surroundings of which provided the background for her next children's book, *Under the Chestnut Tree* (1938). Supported by a cast of villagers from Clunbury she also broadcast from the BBC in Birmingham on Shropshire life.

Bred in the tradition of service to the community cherished by country parsons and doctors, she had long been active in the Women's Institute, and during the Second World War was involved in strenuous work for evacuees and other good causes. In 1945 she and her husband retired to Cerne Abbas in Dorset. He died in 1948 and Mrs Gandy returned to her own county of Wiltshire and settled in Aldbourne near Marlborough.

Her children long since grown up and away from home (to see them she visited Iran, Portugal, Libya and the USA) and her energies unabated, Ida now resumed writing. In 1960 she published *Round About the Little Steeple*, a carefully researched social history of her birthplace, Bishops Cannings, which was followed in 1963 by *Staying with the Aunts*, a vivid account of her father's family and in particular of her five maiden aunts, survivors from the Victorian age, who lived together and kept their coachman and carriage into the 1920s.

Ida was now approaching eighty but still books came. Her passion for the unspoilt Shropshire landscape led in 1970 to *An Idler on the Shropshire Borders*, a nostalgic volume of description and reminiscence. Her last book, *The Heart of a Village*, about the past and present of Aldbourne, where she had lived since 1950, appeared in 1975 – her ninetieth year. She died in September 1977.

PART ONE

CHAPTER I

Introduction to the Village

E V E R Y year thousands of people travelling along the highroad from Marlborough to Devizes look down into the Pewsey Vale and see, rising among the elms at the extreme western end, a tall tower and spire. Even now, when a line of huge pylons rears to the south, the church still dominates the landscape. Nothing can rob her of her grace, and the downs that fold her gently in on three sides add to her dignity and importance. This is St Mary's, parish church of Bishops Cannings, and she has stood there for close on 800 years.

For Bishops Cannings is an ancient parish. It was a rich manor in Domesday time and probably long before. The neighbouring market town of Devizes had not even been heard of in those days. And it is large as well as old, if one thinks in terms of acreage rather than of population—the second largest in the whole of Wiltshire. Even in its present truncated form it still comprises nearly 9,000 acres, and if you want to beat the bounds for yourself you must walk a good thirty miles over the hills and round the southern lowlands.

Let us suppose that you start from the easternmost corner at the big enclosure beside the Marlborough road at Beckhampton and go westwards. You will take the Roman Road as it marches up hill and down dale to Bath, will follow it through high open country between groups of barrows and solitary barrows till it joins company with the imposing post-Roman earthwork of Wansdyke. Here you are looking down into the valley of the Marden, tributary of the Bristol Avon, and at as much of the tiny, secret village of Calstone as chooses to show of itself. You leave on your left a little wood, sadly bespoiled today, once known as Noah's Ark, and perhaps stop for a moment to stare into the rich dairy and market-garden country that spreads below you to the west. Now you are on a little road (a chalk-white road in my childhood, which on old maps is called 'The Calneway') and follow it a few hundred yards northwards. But soon you leave it and strike out along the edge of the wide upland of Roundway Down, where the Royalists beat the Parliamentarians so thoroughly in 1643 that it was nicknamed Runnaway Down. Dropping gradually some 300 feet through cornlands you reach the Devizes-Marlborough road. Turn off it you can (but the Army is in occupation and it will be difficult) just east of the Barracks, take tortuous bends through the 'Floody' and 'Miry' meadows of the old Court Books, round some little boggy copses known as Lea or Lay Woods and cross the doomed Kennet and Avon Canal. Turning westwards again you reach Clay Hole, where they dug great quantities of clay for making the canal at the end of the eighteenth century. Above you is the ridge from which Sir William Waller bombarded Devizes, and beside you the wide pastures of Coate Field, where James I watched a game of football and listened to 'bucolics', through the enterprise and enthusiasm of George Ferebe, then vicar of Bishops Cannings. After Clay Hole the boundary takes you under the dramatic hump of Etchilhampton Hill. You leave Coate on your left and a field called Whittah and drop once more into water meadows, where you cross the young Avon and the footpath to All Cannings. A northward turn brings you once more to the canal (if you want to follow the parish boundary strictly you must swim it, but there is a bridge 100 yards or so away). Once on the other side, a steady climb under Allington Knowle and over the Pewsey road leads you back to the downs. Here you meet the old Saxon military road known as the Harepath and see some well-marked lynchets on your left. The boundary runs over the eastern shoulder of Tan Hill, once so famous for its big and ancient sheep-fair; but Bishops Cannings cannot claim its summit. That is in All Cannings.

Here you are nearly 900 feet up, on that splendid line of downs that stretch from Martinsell on the east to Olivers Camp on the west. There is no more exhilarating bit of country in all Wiltshire. Pewsey Vale, with its copses, its streams, its close-packed trees, its villages and hamlets, all bound in on the south by the long exciting line of Salisbury Plain, is below you. The dark gulf of Wansdyke, that still obstinately withholds the secret of its origin, cuts clean across your path as it runs west to the ancient city of Verlucio and east Savernake. Now, setting your face steadily northwards, you plunge through a lonely sea of downs till you find yourself back where you started, with the pines of Beckhampton singing in your ears. During your long walk you will have passed by, or close to, some ninety barrows of many kinds. For there was once a time when this lonely bit of country was among the most populated in Britain. But on your own walk you may well not have met more than a dozen people.

Throughout this imaginary journey you have been circling round the tall spire of St Mary's and have caught glimpses of it over and over again as it thrusts up above the trees, above the water meadows, above the curving uplands.

Of the thousands who pass along the highroad only a fraction drop down to the village, but those who do so may be fascinated to know that they will be following in the footsteps—if R. J. C. Atkinson is right, and he gives excellent reasons for his belief—of processions of sweating, struggling men, who, somewhere round the year 1500 B.C., dragged behind them huge sarsen stones from the neighbourhood of Avebury on their way to Stonehenge. The stones, he thinks, were 'cradled in massive timbers or bound on enormous sledges',[1] and these journeys probably continued for ten years or more.

It may be that bit of pre-history is too remote to tempt the hurrying motorists, but at the foot of the hill the church offers its own rich reward to anyone ready to spare an hour. He enters by the beautiful canopied south door, ornamented with a pattern of oak-leaves and of ball-and-leaf moulding, goes through a vaulted porch and finds himself in an exceptionally fine and spacious building, a cathedral in miniature. Here is no gloom, no darkness. Light streams from the triple lancets of the big west window, and the traceried clerestory. Only the long chancel is shadowy. Through the open north and south doors (which are indeed nearly always wide open) the air streams in freely.

And this lightness and airiness combine with a sense of massive strength. The great twelfth century pillars look as though they will still be standing in another 800 years, and the kings and bishops under the roof will stare down on generations yet to come.

Of certain features—of the mysterious old box-chair in the southern transept, of the Ernle chapel, of the bells and the organ —more will be said later.

Here I am only attempting a bird's-eye view of church and parish. There is one detail, however, to which I would draw attention. When you pass through the porch you will see a black board with gilt lettering (newly painted by the inn-keeper because the old letters were fading away) which bears the names of the vicars of the parish from John 'Vicaris de Canynges' in 1290 down to the present day. Notice particularly those of George and Thomas Ferebe, two brothers, who held the living between them for fifty-seven years (1593 to 1650). They—but George more particularly— are essential figures in the picture that I shall try to reconstruct of Bishops Cannings in the seventeenth century. George, described by John Aubrey as 'an ingenious man and an excellent musician', was the parson already referred to who entertained both James I and his wife.

There is another feature of the church which must be mentioned now because up to some fifty years ago it played an important part in the traditional character of Cannings. This is the squat little steeple that nestles against the NE side of the spire. A long time ago, the inhabitants won a reputation for being exceptionally simple, and the most widely current of all the stories illustrating their simplicity relates to this little steeple. Its apparent absurdity provided the people in surrounding villages and in Devizes with an excellent excuse for teasing, since they saw it as something as childish and immature as those who lived beneath it. Driven by shame and exasperation, the inhabitants are reported to have carried up a load of manure and planted it round the stones. Then, when the grass began to grow freely they dragged a calf up the steep spiral staircase to eat it down. And in the latter part of the nineteenth century it was still the fashion at Devizes market to greet a Cannings man with derisive laughter and such questions as, 'Hast dunged thy little steeple yet?' or 'Beant it time to dung 'un again?'

In my own childhood the roadman would forestall any jokes at his expense when a traveller stopped to ask the name of the village by replying, 'That's Bishops Cannings—where us dunged the little steeple.'

Yet in spite of all the gibes that small steeple is no odd irrelevant addition. It looked down on the world some 200 years before the spire,[2] and serves its own proper purpose of providing an exit from the spiral staircase. Therefore it should be treated with the respect that it deserves. Just as the true native of Bishops Cannings is shrewder than he first appears so there is more to the little steeple than strikes the casual observer.

How it came about that Cannings people acquired their reputation it is hard to say. Certainly in George Ferebe's time they enjoyed a far different one, since Aubrey wrote: 'The parish in those days would have challenged all England for music, football and ringing'—activities which undoubtedly require intelligence. Perhaps the vicars who succeeded the Ferebes were less lively, less able to give a lead, and so gradually the isolation of the village told on its inhabitants. By the end of the eighteenth century, at all events, it seems as if their character had been firmly fixed, because by that time the famous story of the Moonrakers was widely current.

In an amusing letter to a West Country magazine in 1791[3] a Poulshot farmer claims them for his own village. But the most authoritative opinion assigns them to Bishops Cannings.[4] Not only would one of the many lonely dew-ponds in the parish be an admirable place for the secret dumping of kegs of spirit, brought from the coast by ancient trackways, but the smugglers could also trade on their reputation for stupidity when they assured the Excise men that they were only fishing 'for that girt cheese down in the water'. On that occasion they showed their natural cunning and hood-winked the officers beautifully.

But Cannings tales often do reveal childish simplicity or lack of foresight. There is the cooper who set his small son to hold up the lid of the cask he was making, and was dumbfounded when a small voice cried from within, 'Eh, vayther, how be I to get out?' There was old Farmer Sloper (who lived in the half-timbered farmhouse opposite the church) who put an ailing lamb to revive in too warm an oven and when he took it out and saw its lips curled up, remarked, 'Thee ood'nt grin like that if I hadn't a kept 'ee nice and warm.' There was the man who, sitting on a bough, sawed off the wrong end, and was much taken aback when he landed 'with an almighty bump' on the ground. There was the carter who borrowed his master's waggon in order to take his family to 'The Vize' (an old name for Devizes still in use in the nineteenth century) to see an eclipse of the moon—and many another who acted in an equally absurd fashion.

The tale of the drum-maker is less well known. It is a good instance of the inability of the old Cannings man to look too far ahead. In the early nineteenth century a firm of musical instrument makers in Devizes, named Bruton, was commissioned to make a drum for the Bishops Cannings Friendly Society and, as one of their men lived there himself and was also the village drummer, it was arranged that he should carry out the job on the spot. In the upper room of the old Crown Inn (not the present building) he made a large and splendid drum, painted it handsomely in green, yellow and black. Inside it he wrote: 'Lo, what an entertaining sight are brethren that agree; Brethren whose cheerful hearts unite in bands of piety," followed by the words: 'May the Friendly Society of Bishops Cannings ever flourish! 1820.'

But when the time came to remove it, great was the drum-maker's consternation to find it too wide to pass through either window or door. However, he made the best of a bad job. When, henceforth, the members of the Friendly Society 'walked the village', resplendent in sashes of azure silk tied round their black coats, and carrying silken banners that depicted touching scenes of the succour of the old and sick, he would hurry to the Crown and, standing beside the open window of the upper room, hammer the drum with all his might. This famous drum, after many vicissitudes, including its liberation when the old inn was pulled down, lives once more at the Crown. The day of the gay, genial old Friendly Societies is, alas, over, but the drum still takes a part, even though a lesser one, in village festivities and is always played at a football match on Christmas Bank Holiday; also on such a great occasion as the crowning of the young Queen. In spite of its funny history, nobody may speak slightingly of it. A drummer in a crack regiment tried it himself and pronounced it 'an instrument of rare quality'.

Sometimes a ghostly element creeps into Cannings tales. Early in the nineteenth century the inhabitants of a certain cottage found themselves hypnotised into the most mad and foolish actions by a strange voice.[5] One man threw himself from the top of a ladder while haymaking in the field just behind the house and broke both legs. Years went by and another, a newcomer to the neighbourhood, jumped from a window and had to be treated for shock. The story was forgotten till again the cottage was let to strangers, a mother and daughter; this girl was the third victim. She drank a pint of paraffin and leaped into the well. And always the reason given was the same— '*He* told me to.'

In the little lane that leads from Bishops Cannings to Horton and used to tunnel under overhanging hazels, a ghostly black sow ran wild when twilight fell. Small wonder that no children would go that way at night, for their mothers had warned them what to expect. They themselves had received similar warning from *their* mothers and so on down to the great-grandmothers. The hedgerows on either side are cut low now, the lane is open to the sky, and the terrible sow is seen no more. But she survives in the memories of some who have long left the village.

At the end of the nineteenth century there were still some notably simple inhabitants. Old Eliza Vowle, descendant of an ancient Cannings' family (there was an Elizabeth Vowle in Thomas Ferebe's time) who went about wrapped in an ancient Paisley shawl with white hair streaming from under her bonnet, was the target for many a joke. The village boys teased her unmercifully, yet loved her too. Because she hated to be alone after dark they often sat with her in the evenings, and, to add a little liveliness to the occasion, from time to time when her back was turned they tied strings to the legs of the chairs and passed them under the door to a boy outside. 'Then,' one of them, now an old man, confided to me, 'we'd blow out the tallow candle and there'd only be the moonlight shining down the chimney. And when all the chairs started moving about, Eliza'ud say for a charm, "Lord Jimminy save us!" Leastways thats how it sounded to us. Or we'd string up her old grandfather clock, and when the hands began a-whirlin' round and round she's think it was bewitched, and call in the travelling clockmaker when next he came that way.' Afterwards, when all was peaceful, the boys made her sing to them, 'for she had a wunnerful sweet little voice like a bird's, and 'twas always either "Oh, where and oh where is my Highland laddie gone", or for a hymn, 'twas the first in the book, "Now that the daylight fills the skies".' Sometimes the tricks played on her were more disturbing. Once a baby donkey, stealthily introduced into her cottage at night when she was in bed, made such a racket below that she thought it was the devil himself. When daylight revealed the little creature lying asleep on the hearthrug, she fondled it and bore no ill-will. She allowed none of these tricks to frighten her unduly. She would mumble something, half prayer and half incantation, and go to sleep again.

Just as neither the moonrakers nor the little steeple were in fact as laughable as they seemed, so it was with many Cannings people. Late in the last century a certain Wilts County Councillor, a dapper, monocled gentleman, always deeply concerned at the ignorance of children living in isolated districts, called one afternoon at a lonely farm on Roundway Down. A red-haired boy leaned idly over the gate. The County Councillor at once fired a number of questions at him. 'What is your name? Where do you go to school? What parish do you live in?' Such was the manner of his bombardment.

Not a syllable came from the boy's lips. At the next meeting of the Education Committee, the County Councillor, more worried than ever, gave a sad account of his experience. The boy was clearly little better than an idiot; undoubtedly there must be many more like him. My father listened attentively, recognized the description of the farm and next day made his way there. The boy, no doubt a frequent absentee from school, was again beside the gate.

'Well, Tommy,' says my father, 'so I hear you had a visitor last week?'

'Ah, zur, an zo I did. There come a gentleman with a glass stuck in his eye. He had a little stick in his hand and he stood here a-twirlin' and a-twirlin' of it and axed I a lot of questions.'

'Why didn't you answer him?'

'Lor' bless you, zur, t'warn't worth my while! I zeed straight away a' warn't quite right in his 'ead,' was Tommy's reply.

NOTES TO CHAPTER I

[1] R. J. C. Atkinson, *Stonehenge*.
[2] Ponting, *W. A. M.* XXIII.
[3] *The Western Counties Magazine*, March, 1791.
[4] See H. C. Brentnall, *W.A.M.* XLVIII. 466, and Rev. A. C. Smith, *W.A.M.* XIV. Rev. A. C. Smith writes (in 1853): 'There are certain retired villages in the heart of the downs of N. Wilts . . . whose whole population some seventy years ago were employed in little else.' (i.e. smuggling.)
[5] B. H. Cunnington had this tale from his father. See *W.A.M.* L.

CHAPTER II

George Ferebe

SINCE it was the 'ingenious' parson, George Ferebe, who brought fame to Bishops Cannings during the first quarter of the seventeenth century, the period with which this book is chiefly concerned, it seems fitting to start with some account of him and his family.

He was the eldest son of Thomas Ferebe, a mercer of Cirencester and of his wife Elizabeth (née Hopkins) and was born in 1573. This date is taken from university records.[1] For some unknown reason his baptism does not appear in the registers of St John's Church, possibly because in any case entries were irregular at that early date and the curate-in-charge (William Aldworth, Fellow of Magdalen College, Oxford) was nearing his death-bed, or because extensive repairs to the church were being carried out just then. Hockaday tells us that in 1570 the chancel roof was so ruinous that 'sometimes for a year no one can sit there because of the rain'. So it may be that George was baptized in the little old church of St Lawrence.

He was one of a family of five. His sister Elizabeth was born a year before him, and he was followed by three brothers; John, Thomas, and Anthony. The Ferebes (who spelt their name in thirty-six different ways[2]) were well-to-do people, as may be seen from their wills,[3] and possessed their own coat-of-arms—'a cheffron between three leopards erased,' which was used by two cousins of George Ferebe's on farthing tokens.[4]

Perhaps there was no finer place to grow up in in the whole of sixteenth century southern England than Cirencester, usually spelt Cicester or Cissyter in those days and, indeed, well on into the nineteenth century. As Corinium (i.e. the town on the Corin or Churn), set at the junction of three great roads, it had been for a time under the Romans the largest town in Britain. Though it could no longer claim that distinction it was still exceedingly flourishing and renowned far and wide for the silk and wool that largely provided its 3,500 inhabitants with their livelihood.

Leland, writing about 1540, says: 'Cirencester hath the most celebrate market in all the Quarters on Monday.' On the wide upland pastures round the town wandered great flocks of the famous Cotswold merino sheep, bringing wealth to such noted families as the Chedworths, the Avenings, and many others. The waters of the Churn and its tributaries kept numerous clothing mills, fulling mills and gig mills turning busily, and Thomas Ferebe and his brothers well supplied with goods. Durable and beautiful houses of Cotswold stone, undimmed by age or dirt, lined the streets, and new ones were rising all through George Ferebe's boyhood. His father (as we know by his Will) owned three houses in 'St Ciceley's Street' (now Cicely Hill) and two in Chipping Street (now Dyer Street) adjoining the market place. One of these latter houses he had 'latelie builded' before he died, but his children would have been born in the one 'having the shambles on the left side'—that is, just where Dyer Street begins at the end of the market place.

The very house, now pulled down, is shown, I think, in an old picture, painted before the extensive alterations of 1825-30, that hangs in Cirencester museum. Chipping Street was a distinguished one in which to live, full of fine half-timbered and gabled dwellings occupied by important families. Under its cobbles were buried Roman pavements not unearthed till the mid-nineteenth century. George, an imaginative boy and a lover of the classics, would have been thrilled to know that as he went to and fro to school, strange sea-beasts, Ceres with hair wreathed in corn, Medusa of the snaky locks, Silenus rising from the sea, all lay below him.

I think we may take it for granted that he attended the old grammar school, situated in this same street, since in order to enter Magdalen College he must have been 'completely instructed in reading'. In his early boyhood certain prominent townsmen testified before the Bishop of Gloucester that 'our school at Cyrencester is well, tidily and decently kept . . . and our schoolmaster, named Anthony Ellys, a bachelor of Arts, is a sufficient, meet, well-approved and hable man to teach grammar; and teacheth his

scholars (at that date numbering about 100) dilligently'.[5] The
scholars were sons of the gentry living in and around Cirencester,
and of well-to-day townsmen. Possibly they included, even if only
for a short time, a boy, born in the same year as George Ferebe
himself, who some thirty years later was destined to attend the
entertainment provided for Queen Anne by Ferebe on Cannings
down. This was Henry Danvers, later Earl of Danby, younger son
of Sir John Danvers, an important local landowner,[6] and Lord of
the Manor of Oaksey.

Cirencester was a place to quicken a boy's imagination. To begin with there was the magnificent church of St John. Its tall
pinnacled tower, built of stones that held the light and glowed
even more richly at sunrise and sunset, would have been always
visible from George's home. By the time he was old enough to
care for such things, its interior had been restored and he must
often have wandered and worshipped in it. Here, too, he would
have listened to many a lengthy sermon (such as he himself delivered in later days), from the graceful stone pulpit with its gaily
painted pattern of green and red and gold flowers. Though he
probably was not present when in 1597 a curate preached from
9 a.m. till past 12 o'clock, followed by a second man who went
on for another two hours, his father and brothers would have
been. Protests were made by the victims and the curate 'inhibitted
to use the like for Easter'. Perhaps it was after this that the churchwardens put up the hour-glass that still hangs behind the pulpit.
Whether St John's possessed an organ during George's boyhood is
uncertain, but undoubtedly one existed earlier, when part of the
endowment of the old chapel of St Christopher was used to maintain an organ player. At all events he could listen to a variety of
instruments and it is reasonable to suppose that, as a future
chorister of Magdalen, he sang in the choir. In order to enter the
college as a demy (which according to Aubrey he did) it was required that he should be 'completely instructed' in plain song.
Sometimes, perhaps, he accompanied his father to meetings of the
townsmen in the splendid South Porch.

Not only was Cirencester growing more and more attractive
during these latter years of Elizabeth's reign by the addition of
comely houses, but after all the turmoil and sadness that followed
the dissolution of its monastery, life was growing more serene and

normal. Labour conditions improved and increased prosperity came both to agriculture and to the weaving trade. Above all, the reformed Church began to feel surer of herself and the clergy were no longer so severely torn between the old loyalties and the new. Thomas Ferebe, the prosperous mercer, could decide to send his three eldest sons to Oxford to become parsons without misgiving.

During those early years the young George, always a lively, adventurous person, had leisure to explore the neighbouring countryside, perhaps in the company of his brother John, born three years after him. Thomas and Anthony were too young to join them.

Among the places that they must have visited was the Church of All Saints at North Cerney, standing enchantingly on a wooded hillside some three miles from Cirencester. For here a possible connection of their own, Thomas Fereby, had been rector from 1408 till 1414, and a memorial stone in the chancel asked them to pray for his soul.[7] Later, the unusual octagonal stone pulpit, decorated with a band of 'Cotswold Lily' design, may have linked itself in George's mind with the very similar one at Magdalen College. On the outside of the Church the manticore[8] and the leopard cut boldly on the walls, would delight any child. At Ampney St Mary, the little church set in the fields on the other side of Cirencester, were more strange beasts. Over a Norman doorway, not closed up in their day, the lion of righteousness tramples the wicked serpent underfoot. And at Ampney Crucis was buried, when George was eleven, the good Mr Lloyd, who worked hard on behalf of the Grammar School. You may see him in the church with his wife Anne, and his seven daughters wearing high-crowned beaver hats, and his five curly-headed sons.

Stratton was another little church very close at hand with Ferebe connections, for in it George's cousin and namesake was married. And here again were lions—lions above the door, and Daniel, with a wide, absurd face, like a child's drawing, sitting among them.

On an October day in 1589, a year after the bells of the parish church[9] rang out the defeat of the Armada, George, now sixteen, said goodbye to his native town and its rich countryside and set off along Akerman Street to take up the life of a scholar and a 'pleb fillii' at Magdalen College, Oxford.

OXFORD

Thomas Platter, writing his *Travels in England* ten years after George Ferebe came to Oxford, says of it: 'This town has a most delightful situation, it is not very large, and the colleges occupy most of the site. From the ruined towers and walls one can assume that it was once a strong armed and fortified town. Now, however, it has no great importance, for as noted already, all such things have fallen into decay.'

But young George Ferebe would look at it with other eyes. The ruined towers and walls mattered little to him; the colleges would be everything. Above all, his gaze would go straight to the beautiful tower at the end of High Street—the tower round which his life would centre for the next three years, the tower that crowned what James I declared 'the most absolute building in Oxford'.

When George arrived there the high reputation that Magdalen originally held had fallen greatly during the twenty-eight years of Lawrence Humphrey's Presidency (1561-1589). Education was neglected and discipline slack.[10] But fortunately for Ferebe the old President was replaced about six months later by Nicholas Bond, who soon restored the college's reputation. One of his new rules was that all conversation must be in Latin, and when some doubted whether this rule was kept, he replied that 'scholars dare not presume' to talk anything else. Twice he was made Vice-Chancellor of the University, and altogether 'he seems to have been an able governor both of his own college and of the University, and to have inspired respect and admiration'. Under his guidance Magdalen ceased for a while to have a Puritan bias. He too entertained Queen Elizabeth in 1592, so almost certainly George Ferebe was among the crowd of under-graduates who watched the ceremony.

Though he entered Magdalen as a chorister, this was because he was a potential scholar rather than because his voice, at sixteen, would have been of much use. The average age of choristers had been increasing since 1564, and the sixteen endowments provided for them were used to open the door wider for boys of special ability. Four years after he came to Oxford, Nicholas Bond could no longer bear the loss of young voices, and the age dropped to ten or eleven. But during his last year at all events, George would have been singing in the choir, in a surplice of 'lockeran', and have helped to swell the old pagan hymn to Flora at 4 o'clock on May Day morning on top of Magdalen Tower. Some three years after he came to Oxford his brother John joined him as a chorister at Magdalen.

Among his contemporaries was another musical boy, John Milton, father of the poet, and during part of his time he over-lapped with two other Ferebes ('Ferribie' they spelt their name) belonging to the Yorkshire branch of the family. Moreover, it was at Oxford that George made an important friend—Sir William Knollys, son of Sir Francis, Vice-Chamberlain to Queen Elizabeth. Sir William, in George's own words, 'extended a hand of bounty' to him and gave him and his brothers much encouragement in their studies.[11] The Knollys family had been closely linked with Magdalen for some years. According to Anthony Wood, Francis was a commoner there, and it is likely that William and some of his brothers were too. An early President was possibly an ancestor.

Why the Oxford M.P. and future Comptroller of the Royal Household marked out the Cirencester mercer's son for special favour is entirely guesswork, but I like to think that it was because even then George showed the ingenuity and liveliness that distin-guished him later. At any rate the friendship of Sir William stood him in good stead.

On June 5, 1593, he was ordained at Salisbury by Bishop Cold-well[12] and soon afterwards Sir Michael Ernle of Whetham, near Calne, appointed him to the living of Bishops Cannings, when he was still only twenty. Hugh Gough, the previous vicar, had de-cided to move to All Cannings, three miles to the east, after twenty-nine years in his earlier parish. The Ernles had been Lords of the Manor of Bourton, a hamlet at the eastern end of Bishops Cannings, for several generations, and Michael himself lived there until he married the heiress of the Finnemores. Again it is likely that the Magdalen connection brought George his good fortune. Sir Michael's brother, Francis, went to Magdalen Hall, and so did two of his grandsons, and there was close connection between the two colleges.

The newly-appointed young vicar received permission to miss three terms for 'clerical duties' before he took his M.A.,[13] packed up his books and clothes, said goodbye to his friends, and prepared to begin life in a remote village in the heart of the Wilt-shire Downs.

GEORGE FEREBE COMES TO CANNINGS

If he went straight from Oxford, George would have travelled by first one carrier cart and then another through the Vale of the White Horse and the little old town of Swindon, on over the downs, past the mysterious stone circles at Avebury, and so have entered his own parish when he crossed the Roman Road at Beck-hampton. Or, if as seems more likely, he went home first, then his father would lend him a man and a couple of pack-horses to carry his possessions. In that case we may imagine him starting for Bishops Cannings on a day of late summer. Hugh Gough left the village before Michaelmas, 1593, since he was baptising a young Gough (probably his own by a late marriage) at All Cannings on that day. Proceeding due south from Cirencester Ferebe would cross the low-lying country of the upper Thames, and pass close to the little village of Poole Keynes, where ten years later his brother John became Rector. When he had climbed to the small market town of Wootton Bassett, raised above a mass of trees, he would see before him the long escarpment of the North Wilts downs—whose wide downs that were to flow round him for the rest of his life. Perhaps he ascended them by Broad Town and journeyed on to Bishops Cannings through two other villages (also linked with the Bassett family), Winterbourne and Berwick Bassett. Or he may have turned off towards Calne and have spent a night with his patron in his fine Tudor house at Whetham. Then the last stage of his journey would bring him up Blacklands (or 'Bucklands') Hollow, to the top of the downs, over the Roman Road and Wansdyke, into the N.W. corner of his parish, and along the old chalk 'Calneway'—now a metalled road cutting through golflinks: on his left rose the fine upland of Morgan's Hill, cul-minating in the little upstanding 'Vuzz Knowle', and straight across his path the Bath to London coaching road ran level from the west after its astonishing climb up Bagdon Hill. It was along this famous old road that twenty years later Queen Anne came driving from Bath to London.

On his right stretched Roundway Down, completely within

the bounds of his parish, unploughed, thick with sheep, and probably houseless. Here he perhaps stopped to chat to a shepherd and found him one of his new flock. But, whichever way he travelled to Bishops Cannings, he looked down on it at last from the same spot a hundred yards or so below the junction of the 'Calneway' with the ancient 'Harepath'. At this cross-roads stood, I believe, the 'Cannings Heard' (or 'Hand') Cross of the seventeenth century Court Books. It was an important spot in those days, when the road from Devizes followed the line of the present fir plantation above Westend and joined the other two roads just here. A traveller to Marlborough would follow the Harepath up under Morgan's Hill till he joined the coaching road.

At Cannings Hand Cross a track led down to the village. The present Hollow was not dug till the early nineteenth century, so Ferebe's family never knew the joy, experienced by later children, of tunnelling deep into the snow when it filled the Hollow from bank to band. As he stands just below the Cross, where the whole Pewsey Vale sweeps into view, we may imagine him stopping for a good look at his new domain. The crowning point, of course, is the church, springing from an even denser mass of elms than surrounds it today. Delicate and pale, or richly dark, according to the wind, the high uplands of Salisbury Plain next hold his eye, and he pictures himself riding across it to Salisbury.

No canal winds through the intervening lowlands, but the young Avon, free and untapped, flashes out here and there as it runs south-eastward through water meadows. Nearer at hand, below and all about him, are the open fields, where many of his new parishioners will be busily harvesting their strips.

For his entry into the village there would surely be many spectators, and perhaps a few to accompany him down Chandler's Lane to the Parsonage House, situated under the very shadow of the church in the south-western corner of the 3-acre glebe field. The vicarage stood there in 1773, and when pulled down in 1847 it was an exceedingly ancient building, as one of its crumbling oak beams, long preserved in a glass case in the hall of the present vicarage, testified. To a child s eye it used to look like some prehistoric monster. In the new parchment register of 1651, Thomas Ettwall, the vicar who succeeded George Ferebe's brother Thomas, wrote: 'I did new-lay and point the tiles of my house and build

the kitchen and chamber chimneys in the year 1663.' Strengthened
and repaired, it served a succession of vicars for another 180 years.
Already the great chestnut that stood close to this earlier vicarage
must have been quite a well-grown tree. When cut down about
1920 it was around 500 years old.

Those who welcomed Ferebe would include the two churchwardens, Thomas Cook and Robert Dicke. Thomas Cook was
steward to the Bishop of Salisbury for his Manor of Cannings, and
a man of some social standing, since his eldest daughter married
into the old and honoured Roundway family of Nicholas. Robert
Dicke bore a surname that occurs repeatedly in early registers.
The curate, Edward Ashley, in charge of the parish since Hugh
Gough moved to All Cannings, would also be there, and possibly
John Ernle, son of Sir Michael, and now Squire of Bourton.

When Ferebe has been duly welcomed and has visited the
church, we may picture him wandering into the Parsonage Field,
where he will keep his cow, his bees, his geese and hens. It is a
pleasant place today and must have always been so, sunny and
well-drained, with the village nestling close round it. The giant
elm, that used to stand on a little hummock that it had made for
itself, would provide shade on summer days, for even then it was
close on 200 years old. Other elms on the north gave shelter from
the winds that sweep from the downs. Looking east Ferebe would
see a shapely green hill rising boldly against the sky above Easton,
or, nearer at hand, a glance over the hedge revealed the funny
little sunken alley called Pip Lane with its cobble-stones and
possibly the same huddle of cottages, all very ancient, pulled down
early in the present century. To the west of his glebe ran Chandlers' Lane, perhaps even then shaded by limes, and the half-
timbered manor house belonging to the Manor of the Dean and
Chapter.[14]

On the south, separated from the Parsonage Field only by a
ha-ha, lay the churchyard where the Vicar had the right to graze
his sheep. And high above the vicarage, high above the chestnut
tree, towered the splendid church, heart and centre of his future
life.

For at least seven years his first wife, Elizabeth, shared this with
him, though we do not know where she came from or where he
married her.[15] She bore him three children. The first, named after

her, was baptized in 1601. Then came two boys, both, in the
muddling fashion of the time, christened Thomas—the elder in
May, 1605, and the second in November, 1608. Six weeks after the
birth of this younger son his mother died, and six months later his
father married Bridget Dugdayle, a Cannings girl, sister or
daughter of a churchwarden in Thomas Ferebe's time. Had George
lived in the eighteenth or nineteenth centuries he might have been
given 'rough music' for not waiting till his first wife had been
dead a full year, as happened to a Cannings inn-keeper in the
1880's. The clash and clang of pots and pans and loud angry voices
filled the midnight air when he brought his second bride to the
old inn beside the churchyard.

Though George was only thirty-six at the time of his marriage
to Bridget no further children were born. When he had been vicar
of Cannings for eighteen years his father died, and it seems likely
that his mother came to live with him. I feel pretty sure that she
was the widow, Elizabeth Ferebe, whom Thomas buried at Cannings in 1634.

The Cirencester mercer gave George nothing but the 'black
mourning suit' which all four sons were to receive. As a shrewd
business man he evidently felt that this eldest son, vicar of a comparatively wealthy parish,[16] stood in no need of financial help.
His youngest son, Anthony, carrying on the family business, must
have the bulk of his fortune when proper provision had been made
for his widow.[17]

Certainly there is every reason to believe that the thirty years
George spent in his vicarage beside the church were secure and
happy. Since he was popular with his people his barn was likely
to be kept well filled. Moreover, when he had been at Cannings
seven years Sir Thomas Edward appointed him to the living of
Calstone. It was only three miles across the downs and meant an
extra £35 in his pocket. His university education and his personal
gifts ensured him a good social position. Such a highly respected
Devizes townsman as John Drew was his close personal friend, and
Sir William Knollys remained his patron. His curate, Edward
Ashley,[18] made it possible for him to preach both elsewhere in the
diocese and beyond it. Richard Berkeley, writing from Stoke
Gifford in 1625 to offer Thomas Ferebe another living, says: 'I

have very often heard your Brother preach at Bath and at Brad-ford both.'[19]

And since there was no need for him to labour in his glebe George had ample time to train his people to play and sing with the noteworthy success that they scored twenty years after his arrival in the parish.

NOTES TO CHAPTER II

[1] Oxford University Register (Clark) and Alumni Oxoniensis.

[2] I have adopted the spelling used in Sir T. Phillipps' *Wilts Institutions*. George himself uses three different spellings in the Parish Registers.

[3] The Will of George Ferebe (uncle) in Gloucester Probate Office and of Thomas (father) in Somerset House, P.C.C.

[4] Edmund Feriby issued one between 1650-1672 (it is undated), and George Ferebee one in 1666. (Information supplied by J. N. Taylor, Glos. City Museum.)

[5] For this quotation and other information I am indebted to Badderley's *History of Cirencester*. The master's stipend, originally only £7, was increased to £20 in 1583 through the efforts of the wealthy, Welsh-born George Lloyd.

[6] Sir John bought the Manor of Oaksey in 1563 (the site of Cirencester House) and built himself a Tudor mansion. Though he also spent some of his time on his Wiltshire estate of Dauntsey and Henry was actually born there, we know that he was often at Cirencester later on, because of the vigorous quarrel he carried on with a certain rebellious local tradesman who disputed his manorial rights.

[7] *The Ancient and Present State of Gloucestershire* (1712) by Sir Robert Atkyns. The stone is no longer there. This may well be the same Thomas (given as 'clerk') who, with two other Gloucestershire men, makes over a grant of land in Essex to Thomas, Duke of Gloucester, in 1395 (Hist. M.S.S. Vol. IV. 330). This priest also took part in other land transactions in Essex in the latter half of the fourteenth century (Printed Feet of Fines for Essex Vol. III). Two other possible ancestors were William de Ferriby, rector of Minchinhampton in the second half of the fourteenth century, and also the more important secular founder of Chipping Campden Grammar School in 1486, John Verby (or Feriby), whose bust is set over the stone fireplace in the old class-room.

[8] A fabulous beast with the head of a man and the body of a lion.

[9] The eight bells were *recast* a few years before the Civil War. (Badderley.)

[10] Humphrey, though a distinguished scholar, seems to have shown more interest in feathering his own nest (he was the first married President) than in looking after the welfare of the college. He was an enthusiastic Puritan who hated dressing himself up either in ecclesiastical vestments or academic robes. But when Queen Elizabeth visited Oxford he overcame his scruples sufficiently to put on his scarlet gown. She chaffed him about it, saying: 'Dr. Humphrey, methinks your gown and habit become you

very well and I marvel you were so straight-laced on this point.' H. A. Wilson, *History of Magdalen College* (to which I owe other details here given).

[11] *Vide* Ferebe's Dedication to Sir W. Knollys in Ferebe's sermon *Life's Farewell*. (See p. 113 below.)

[12] The Bishop's Registers for 1593. Diocesan Registry, Salisbury. There is no mention of his later ordination as priest.

[13] Oxford University Register (Clark).

[14] See Ch. VI.

[15] I have failed to trace this marriage either in the Cirencester registers, or in those of adjoining villages, or at Oxford.

[16] In 1649 the tithes amounted to £421 for corn, wool, lambs and hay. A tenth part of those for lambs and wool went to the vicar, as well as his share of wheat and barley, and the money from such glebe land as he did not farm himself. Probably this estimate did not greatly differ earlier in the century.

[17] See Appendix A for the Will of Thos. Ferebe.

[18] Ashley married a Cannings girl and had four children. He signs for the new register in 1601. Much later he seems to have resigned his curacy and to have become a churchwarden.

[19] Q.S.G.R. Ed. B. H. Cunnington, p. 81. Mr Cunnington thought this letter might be a hoax, partly because the living was offered to two men at the same time. But the statement about having heard Thomas' brother preach may be considered genuine, and his 'brother' is definitely more likely to be George than John.

CHAPTER III

The Church and the Bells

THE CHURCH

IT WAS Bishop Jocelyn of Salisbury who in all probability started St Mary's Church before he became a Cistercian monk in 1184. When he undertook the task he was building on the foundations of a still older church, fragments of which were detected in the walls before the big restoration of 1880.[1]

The Bishop would naturally want to see a church worthy of his own large rich manor. Though there have, of course, been many alterations, St Mary's remains essentially the same today as when George Ferebe entered it for the first time—perhaps for his institution or perhaps on an earlier visit. There was the same loftiness, the same massive pillars with their bold and pleasing capitals, the same long twilit chancel. But in place of the stone altar at the end, the handsome Elizabethan oak table now in the Ernle chapel stood, most likely, in the nave below the central arch.

The Ernle chapel in the south transept, once dedicated to St Clement, but later called 'Our Lady Bowere', had been made over to the Ernle family, thirty years before Ferebe became vicar, by the churchwardens, Thomas Sloper and John Perse. They signed a conveyance[2] granting it to John Ernle, father of Ferebe's patron, Sir Michael, 'as a burying place for him and his heirs forever', provided that they continued to carry out all proper repairs. Hitherto, declared the churchwardens, the Lady Bower had been used 'for the celebration of papistical masses . . . repugnant and contrary to divine law'. But a more practical reason, no doubt, for their action was that they and the vicar, Richard Akers, wanted to rid themselves of one of their many financial responsibilities.

So John Ernle entered into possession, received permission to build pews in the chapel, and was buried there himself in 1571. George Ferebe, exploring the church, would examine with interest the memorial to his patron's father. It is adorned with the stone bust of a knight wearing the long tasselled cap that appears on all old Ernle tombs. Six oak-leaves flow wing-like from his shoulders, and from a delicate design of more oak-leaves below peer a hound and a small pony. Within the recess a little angel looks down. On the front of his tomb the Ernle coat-of-arms with its six flying eagles is repeated three times. Probably the whole was topped by the swarthy Saracen's head, with black bushy eyebrows, black upturned moustaches and pointed beard (memento perhaps of some crusading exploit), that balances now on a rusty helmet above the tomb of John's grandson, Walter of Etchilhampton, on the east wall of the chapel.

Where the exciting and unusual box-chair or carrel, now in the south transept, stood then there is no telling. After the Reformation it may have been moved from its present place to the dark corner beside the belfry door which it occupied in the nineteenth century. Many are the conjectures as to its use and origin. Ferebe and his contemporaries understood far more about it than we do.[3] At all events it remains a strange and exciting object. Though much of the framework is post-reformation, the back panel, whereon is painted a large outspread hand, is far older. The short cheerless sentences, all relating to sin and death, are in fifteenth century lettering. Ferebe, true child of his age and living on easier terms with death, would not find them as gloomy and repugnant as ourselves. When he sat down in his vicarage close by to write a funeral sermon for his friend, John Drew of Devizes, many of the words on the Hand would have been in his mind.

'We must needs die,' was the preacher's text.

'Thou shalt die,' proclaims the Hand.

'Thy life thou canst not lengthen,' it tells us. And Ferebe enlarges dramatically on the fruitlessness of all the efforts to save his friend.

Perhaps his children, wandering round the church while still very young, and seeing the great pale hand gleam from the shadows, thought, as did some Cannings children 400 years later, that it belonged to God. But his nephew Thomas clearly felt no such inhibitions. He boldly scrawled his name on the back panel, for all the world to see. We forgive him because he was only a small boy who lived long ago and knew no better, but indignation rises hotly at sight of other less excusable signatures. Another piece of church furniture belonging to Ferebe's time was the alms-box, cut in one piece from an oak bough, immensely solid and provided with three locks—one for the vicar and two for the churchwardens. Black with age it stands at the western end of the nave.

But for all its beauty, its size, its distinction, St Mary's Church lacked two things that seemed essential to the new parson—an organ and a peal of bells. Though a small band of villagers played their various instruments on Sunday and a solitary bell called the people to church, these failed to fatisfy him. Organs might still be rare in village churches, but he had been accustomed to one at Cirencester and most likely at Magdalen[4] and an organ he must and would have. How soon he achieved one it is impossible to say. We know from John Aubrey that when King James I visited the parish in 1618 'the organ was played on for state'.[5] We know too that in 1602 eight fine bells, in the key of E flat, were cast by the oldest bell-founders in Wiltshire, the firm of John Wallis of Salisbury. Sixty years later John Aubrey claimed that Bishops Cannings could challenge all England for ringing.

His first survey of the Church ended, the young vicar would, I think, have climbed the dark spiral stairs to the top of the tower. When he had passed through the door in the little steeple he looked down on one of the finest views in Wiltshire.

Beyond the upland fields to east and west and north rise the enfolding crescent of the downs, with Tan Hill to relegate them firmly to their proper place. To the south wide water meadows melt into the Pewsey Vale, that stretches on till it encounters the bold barrier of Salisbury Plain. Away on the eastern horizon two little rounded hills—Woodborough and Wilcot Clumps—rise like islands in a blue sea. When, his survey of the landscape ended, he let his gaze travel skywards he would see the same copper weather-cock that tells the wind today. It may be that in the years ahead his children—Bridget, Elizabeth and two Thomases—played touch-last round the spire, like other Cannings children, and found the same excitement when the little steeple imposed its bulk across their path—the funny little steeple doomed to become a butt for all the villages around.

THE BELLS

As has been said, in 1602 eight bells, cast by John Wallis, were hung in the tower of St Mary's. They form the most solid memorial to George Ferebe and a lasting tribute to his energy and enthusiasm. The raising of the necessary money called for tremendous effort. Bell metal in 1592 was worth £2 16s. a cwt., and twenty years later it had risen to double that amount in Wiltshire.[6] Since the weight of the Cannings tenor alone is 17 cwt. (the same as the tenor of Ferebe's old college) we get a good idea of the great sum of money that had to be raised.

John Wallis, the famous Salisbury bell-founder, started work nineteen years earlier—in Culver Street, formerly Bell Founders' Street.[7] The first of all his bells went to Little Bedwyn, twenty miles east of Cannings, and among many others in Wiltshire he supplied the weighty tenor at Great Bedwyn and its fifth bell, unequalled for 'liveliness of tone'. For Salisbury Cathedral he cast eight splendid bells to hang in a separate tower, and two for St John's, Devizes. But Bishops Cannings beat the town by eight years.

John Wallis loved to engrave short religious mottoes or texts on his bells. 'Be meeke and holy to heare the word of God' proclaims a Little Bedwyn bell. 'Hope well,' says the second Cannings bell, and 'Feare God,' the second. The tenor, because of its greater importance, bears the full message, 'Feare God: Honour the Kinge.' But perhaps there was some flaw in it, for Thomas Ferebe had it recast in 1626.

George Ferebe's name (spelt here as Ferrabe) was set, as well it might be, on the fifth, and Thomas Sloper, senior churchwarden that year, is honoured on the sixth. The little parson's bell (cast by James Brough of Devizes), that hurries late-comers to church, did not join the others till 1738.

So stirring an event as the hanging of eight bells would have been marked, according to custom, by a special service and a village feast. Just such a service took place when the tenor returned after a long absence nearly 300 years later. Early one

Easter morning as the bells pealed across the village an ominous
sound broke harshly on the ear. The great bell had cracked for
the second time in its history. Money must be raised; concerts
and jumble sales organized. Meanwhile the other bells sadly
missed the voice that lent them weight and authority. And when
at last the tenor returned the whole population, whether church
or chapel, gathered together for a service of dedication and thanksgiving. They pressed close to the chancel arch and filled the tran-
septs to watch the blessing of the bell. Then all sang the forty-
second psalm. And now to the straining of ropes and the creak
of machinery, the huge grey form rose slowly, gently swaying,
till it disappeared through the trap-door into the darkness of the
tower. The organ thundered out 'Now thank we all our God'.
Remembering the words of the psalm we had just sung it seemed
to us children that He—or rather His messenger—had indeed
'gone up with a merry noise'. In the biggest barn available everyone sat down to a thanksgiving feast and soon the bells rang out
more joyfully than ever before.

I like to think that something similar happened when the new
bells took their place in the tower. George Ferebe, 'ingenious man'
and ready rhymster, who wrote the verses to honour the Queen's
passing through the parish, would surely have composed a special
hymn for this other, much greater event; only unfortunately no
copy has survived.

Infinite activity lay before the famous peal. Not only would it
call the people to Church on Sundays and on numerous Saints'-
days, year after year, century after century, but many were the
national occasions that it would celebrate in the immediate
future. There was the accession of James I; the foiling of Gun-
powder Plot; the marriage of the king's beautiful young daughter
to the Count Palatine, hope of the Protestant cause in Europe; the
birth of her first two sons, famous fiery Prince Rupert, and Prince
Maurice, who led his men to victory on top of Roundway Down
in 1643. In 1613 they acclaimed Queen Anne's passage through
the parish, and in 1618 that of King James. In 1623 peals went up
from nearly every church tower in England when Prince Charles
returned—unengaged—from his hated matrimonial quest in Spain.
George Ferebe himself did not hear his bells that time. He had been
dead just a month. Whether, in Thomas Ferebe's day, the Can-

nings bells pealed in honour of the Royalist victory on Roundway
Down there is no telling, but the chances are that they did. We
know that when Prince Charles (afterwards Charles II) passed
through Devizes during the Civil War, the Mayor ordered that
the bells should ring till the steeples rocked.[8]

And always, be it remembered, there was extra work for the
tenor. Not only must she continue the call to church when the
others had ceased, and preside at funerals—she must also toll
three times for each man who died, twice for each woman, once
for each child, and for important people, or for those who lived
to be very old, there was an extra stroke for each year of their
lives. Could this custom have helped her to crack twice? Cannings
people live to a great age.

We have no means of knowing definitely whether George
Ferebe's ringers tried their hands at change ringing. Possibly they
did since it was introduced early in the seventeenth century.
Ferebe, keeping in touch with Oxford, may have picked up the
idea from the Societies of 'Youths and Scholars' that met in the
city to practise the new art.[9] Moreover, Aubrey's reference to
Cannings ringing as 'famous throughout all England', looks as
though it was in some way unusual. The earliest book on Change
Ringing[10] was not published till 1668. But interest, stifled during
the Civil War and the Commonwealth, had been growing long
before that, and after the Restoration change-ringing went ahead
rapidly. Travellers to England in the seventeenth century were
amused and surprised by the Englishman's love for bells. Paul
Hentner, a native of Brandenburg, roving this country five years
after George Ferebe's arrival in Cannings, observed that the
English 'are vastly fond of great noises that fill the air, such as
the firing of canon, drums, and the ringing of bells . . . it is
common for a number of them that have got a glass in their heads
('—qui se inebriaverint') to go up into some belfry and ring the
bells for hours together'.

There was no such strange custom where he came from, nor
indeed in any other part of Europe. As for the 'glass in their
heads', it is true that the majority of ringers in all ages have found
it has given them the necessary zest beforehand, and refreshment
afterwards. John Stephens, in his account of Ale Houses, remarks,
'A good Ring of Bells in the parish helps her (the hostess) to many

a taster. She prays the Parson may not be a Puritan.' This Ferebe
certainly was not, nor is it likely that his ringers were an excep-
tion to the general rule. In all likelihood the village pub stood
just where the new one does today, at the very threshold of the
churchyard, on the site of an old thatched inn.

NOTES TO CHAPTER III

[1] At a meeting of the British Archaeological Society of Great Britain in
1880 Mr Brock said that in the walls of Bishops Cannings church he had
found fragments of what he believed to be Saxon work.

[2] Among the Ernle papers at Whetham.

[3] The most acceptable view seems to be that adopted by Archdeacon
Macdonald, which is as follows : A carrel (from *quarrée*=a square box)
was used in pre-reformation times by monks and clergy for private meditation and study, not only in monastic buildings but probably also in large
parish churches, such as Bishops Cannings, closely connected with their
own cathedral. For such a purpose the Hand of Meditation was particularly appropriate. An interesting account of the use of the carrel is given
in *The Rites of Durham Abbey* (Surtees Society Edition, pp. 70, 71). 'The
north side of the cloister . . . was all finely glassed from the hight to the
sole within a little of the ground unto the cloister garth. And in every
window iij pews or carrells, where every one of the old monks had his
carrell . . . when they had dyned they did resorte to that piece of cloister,
and there studyed upon their books, each one in his carrell all the afternoon
unto evensong tyme. And in every carrell was a desk to lye their books
on'—as there is in the Cannings carrell. I believe I am right in saying that
there is now no other quite like it in England, but in the late sixteenth
century there would have been several still in existence.

[4] One bought in 1597 was removed by Oliver Cromwell to Hampton
Court. It is likely that in a College noted in the sixteenth century for its
music this organ had replaced an earlier one.

[5] This organ probably lasted till 1811. See Epilogue.

[6] Rev. C. Lukis, *W.A.M.* III. 52. To him I owe other information in this
Chapter.

[7] The firm of Wallis (later Wallis & Denton, and then the Purdues)
supplied bells to Wiltshire from 1581-1731.

[8] Waylen, *History of Devizes.*

[9] Ernest Morris, *Bells of All Nations.*

[10] Fabian Stedman, *Tintanologia.* He gives his name to a particular
method of change-ringing.

CHAPTER IV

The Parish

THE PARISH AS A WHOLE

THE parish of Bishops Cannings, a very large one today, was
even larger in Ferebe's time. For it included not only the villages
of Cannings, Horton and Coate and the hamlets of Bourton and
Easton, but also that part of Devizes known as the Chapelry of
St James, with its tithings of Roundway, Nursteed, Wick and Bedborough, as well as the distant little village of Chiltoe.

The whole of the village of Bishops Cannings itself is now in
the hands of the Crown, except for the lands of one independent
owner. But for some 500 years before Ferebe's arrival and right on
till it was sold to the Crown in 1858 the greater part of the parish
belonged to the Bishops of Salisbury (save for two short intervals),
and was known as Cannings' Episcopi. A smaller manor, probably
originating in the priest's holding of two hides mentioned in
Domesday (and centering round the Church, vicarage and glebe)
was presented by Bishop Osmund to the Cathedral itself in 1091.[1]
Henceforth this portion, under the title of Cannings Canonicorum,
was the property of the Dean and Chapter. At the end of the sixteenth century and the beginning of the seventeenth it was farmed
by two members of the Weston family—that persistent and prolific tribe—in conjunction later with Thomas Stretche.[2]

During the earlier period covered by this book, John Ernle held
Bourton Manor, and later his stepmother, Lady Susan Reynolds,
farmed it. A survey made in 1634 by Michael Tidcombe,[3] steward
to the Bishop of Salisbury, gives some idea of the way the land in
Cannings was held eleven years after Ferebe's death. In Cannings
Canonicorum 140 acres of arable were divided into 9 yardlands
and 9 tenements, and there were 34 acres of meadow and pasture

for 730 sheep. The rest of the tithing consisted of the tenements of Sir John Danvers—an absentee landlord living at West Lavington, repeatedly fined for failing to attend the meetings of the Manor Court—and of 3 other freeholders, 9 leaseholders, and 5 copyholders. In the manor of Bourton there were 10 freeholders and 12 copyholders, 120 acres of arable, 22 of meadowland and pasture on the downs for 600 sheep.

Enclosure, with all its blessings and its injustices, came late to the parish as to much of the county, partly because there was abundant pasture for sheep without it. In the early seventeenth century not more than five to ten per cent of Cannings land had been enclosed, though now and then an abortive attempt is reported. In 1595 the Hommage of Canning's Canonicorum presents that 'Le Laynes, or South Marsh, have been enclosed without licence'.[4] Not till 1794 was an Act of Enclosure passed (or for Coate in 1778) and though Charcroft, the big common field east of the village shop, was nominally enclosed the villagers continued to graze their beasts there right on into the second half of the nineteenth century.

In the Bishop's Manor the 3-field system was followed; in that of the Dean and Chapter, the 4-field.[5] All over the parish were scattered the open fields, among them the Town Furlong, Charcroft and Broadlands in Cannings; the Picked Land in the Bovill (the land cutting in at the foot of Easton Hill, then called the Bove Hill), Dicklesbury, and Honey Furlong, Gold Furlong and Mareshedge, Long Stonyland, Docklands in Bourton and Easton; the Nettle Hills in Horton; Bystones and Lellands in Coate; Duck Ruddles, Amblecombe and Shillands in Roundway. Some of these names are a sure guide to the nature of the land. In many cases the strips were very small. At Roundway, for instance, the three big fields at the end of the sixteenth century were broken into no less than 160 strips, many of half an acre or less, and this continued into the mid-seventeenth century.[6] And on the downs themselves were the common grazing grounds, including Cockham and Cannings Cow-down.

When Ferebe arrived in Cannings the arable was in a poor state after two bad harvests in succession. The Common Shepherd might move his sheep diligently from field to field, but not even this enrichment of the soil could compensate for the serious shortage of good seed corn. So life was harder than ever both for for the yeoman farmers and the copyholders and freeholders who made up the bulk of the population.

Another shortage occurred in 1608, when petitions were sent to the magistrates from places all over Wiltshire asking that licences might be granted for the purchase of corn to sell again for the use of the poor.[7] Patiently and doggedly, through bad years and good, the Wiltshires, the Merritts, the Baileys (or Bellys), the Slopers (or Slops), the Haslands, the Etwells, and many another old Cannings family, cultivated their widely scattered strips or their small holdings, fought for their rights, exceeded them, lived to an average age of about 50,[8] and were buried first by George and then by Thomas Ferebe under the tall spire.

Year after year the mid-seventeenth century Court Books record the meetings (usually in April or October) of the tenants of the Manor. Unfortunately the existing records of George Ferebe's time are meagre, but in the later years of Thomas Ferebe, when Robert Henley farmed both Bourton and Cannings, his steward kept full records in a beautiful, clear hand. They are representative of the orders and penalties issued all through the earlier part of the century. Year after year the tenants are ordered to mark their boundaries by 'pitching merestones', or making 'mere-balls'. Year after year such people as 'The Widow Julian Paradise' are told to cleanse their ditches before the Feast of St Andrews or to pay a fine of ten shillings. Year after year men get into trouble for over-stocking Cannings Cowdown or for letting their beasts stray into the cornfields. And time after time the Hommage reaffirms that 'none shall bait any horse, beast, or sheep within the cornfields of Cannings, Roundway, Bedborough or Horton' between May 1st and Michaelmas, under a penalty of 3s. for each beast.

Thomas Withers, son of an early churchwarden of George Ferebe's, who has stopped up a public footpath, must pay twelve pence and make it good. Jeffrey Pottenger has failed to place a bridge over his stream.

A keen eye is kept on all houses and barns. Nobody may say: 'This is *my* property and I shall do what I like with it—' far less so than today. When Christopher Potter's barn is blown down by the wind he is ordered to build it again within five months. A widow, whose 'mansion house' is destroyed by fire, is given more timber to rebuild it, and another widow receives timber for repair work. Time and again a little band of men are made responsible for seeing that rights of way and boundaries are properly maintained and foul ditches cleansed. In 1595 John Stephens is in trouble for lopping off the branch of a tree without permission.

As to methods of agriculture, 'sod burning' supplemented the manuring of the land by sheep. The surface of the turf was skimmed off with a breast plough, piled loosely in heaps, lighted at the top and allowed to smoulder. Then, when ploughing was over, seed and ashes were broadcast together. Such a practice too freely followed impoverished the land, but on the downs 'sod-burning' continued for a long time.[9] The plough most favoured in Wiltshire was the heavy western sallow, usually with two wheels but sometimes only one, and for the wetter land a one-footed affair.

Sometimes a weighted thornbush served as a harrow which, provided the soil was dry enough, worked very well. Both horses and oxen were used for ploughing and harrowing, but whereas on the steeper upland fields, such as Dicklesbury or Honey Furlong, horses would have been more popular, for the low-lying fields the ox was considered the better beast. In his attractive *The Secret People*, Mr Martin writes: 'Ploughmen in the fields worked happily in pairs, chanting softly to their oxen in local dialect, with inflexions that the beasts understood. To them the lumbering oxen with their splayed feet and rolling gait were the ideal beasts for ploughing,' and he goes on to quote 'Old Fitzherbert'— 'Therefore, meseemes, all thynges considered, the ploughe of oxen is much more profitable than the plough of horses.' Oxen were cheaper to feed and steadier, even if slower. A few Wiltshire farmers still clung to them even as late as the end of the nineteenth century. I remember, as a small child, climbing up from the canal near Horton and as I scrambled through the hedge meeting the staring, patient eyes of a pair of white oxen yoked to a plough.

Sir Walter Blyth, the seventeenth century writer on agriculture, made the fantastic suggestion that elephants should be employed to help with heavy work on the land, though that was scarcely one to be taken seriously. Cannings husbandmen, like others all over England, would certainly have been slow to adopt any new ideas or methods. This same Sir Walter, lamenting the state of

English agriculture, cries out: 'The fourth and last abuse is a calumniating and depraving of every new invention; of this most culpable are your mouldy old leavened husbandmen. . . . If an improvement is discovered to him and his neighbours, he'll oppose and degrade it. "What forsooth," says he, "who taught you more wit than your forefathers?"[10] So, too, does another writer in the same century, R. Child, complain in his 'Large Letter', 'that men object that the new seeds' (i.e. clover, saintfoin and lucerne)— 'will not grow with them,' and, he goes on, 'To these I reply and ask them, How do they know? Have they ever tryed? Idleness never wants an excuse. And why might not our forefathers upon the same ground have held their hands in their pockets and have said that wheat and barley would not have grown with us?'

And so in Cannings, as all over the county, men confined themselves largely to wheat, barley, and either oats or peas, though possibly some more enlightened farmers started a root crop during Ferebe's later years, and vetches were gradually growing more popular. To be fair to the small holders, their tiny, widely separated, and over-cultivated strips gave them small chance for new experiments. It was perhaps only people like John Ernle of Bourton, or Griffin Nicholas of Roundway, who could afford to try out new crops, though possibly in the southern part of the parish the long belt of greensand that ran right through the Pewsey Vale tempted some of the smaller farmers to experiment.

THE DOWNLANDS

Like most downland parishes Bishops Cannings has its feet in the water meadows and its head high on the hills.

Sheep
In the period of which I am writing by far the larger part of the parish was unploughed grassland given over to sheep. According to Aubrey some 500,000 roamed the Wiltshire downs in the seventeenth century, and Cannings was one of the biggest wool-raising districts in a county producing more wool than any other. When Michael Tidcombe surveyed the Manor in 1634 the flocks of the bigger landowners alone numbered over 2,000. Sir Edward Baynton kept 1,000 sheep, Lady Susan Reynolds (widow of Sir

Michael Ernle) had 600 on Bourton Down, and on Horton Down the 'heir of Simon Unwin' owned pasture for 800. But even these great flocks could not keep pace with the requirements of the Ludlows, the Methuens, the Stumps, the Longs and other famous Wiltshire clothiers. Bishops Cannings itself lay on the fringe of the weaving district and full-time weavers in the parish were never numerous. The sheep who walked the downs on long, strong legs were the old Wiltshire Horned sheep. They walked so energetically that their mutton was excessively tough, but all this exercise combined with the wholesome downland grass kept them remarkably healthy. Aubrey says of them in his *Natural History of Wilts*, 'As to our Wiltshire sheep . . . they are not subject to the shaking which Dorset sheep are. Our sheep about the chalke never die of the rot.' The amount of wool that they carried—with none at all on their bellies—was nothing to boast of. The average weight of a fleece in the early seventeenth century was only about 2 lbs. as compared with 3½ or 4 lbs. today. Aubrey puts the wool of the sheep pasturing in the common fields as the best, but rates downland wool as of secondary quality. Nevertheless, theirs was 'the golden hoof.' Garratt said that they were so excellent a folding breed that Wiltshire then grew more corn than any other of its size.[11]

The movements of the Cannings flocks were most strictly regulated. 'None shall feed their sheep on Cannings Cowdownes from April 25th till Michaelmas' we read over and over again in the seventeenth century Court books. In the autumn they came down to graze in the stubble of each sheep-owning tenant in turn, so that all might reap the benefit of the dung. So highly prized was this that those with no sheep would pay 11d. for the dunging of an acre.[11] Steadily these athletic sheep moved from field to field throughout the winter. And then once more they were driven up the sheep-walks to the high downs, where they kept the turf smooth as a lawn. Paul Hentner speaks of 'the short and tender grass of the downs', and how upon them 'wander numerous flocks extremely white, and whether from the temperature of the air or the goodness of the earth, bearing softer and finer fleeces than those of any other country' (a statement that perhaps some wool experts would have disputed). Aubrey noticed how the downland grass was 'rich and fragrant with thyme and burnet'—as it was in my childhood and still is on certain favoured spots. Incidentally,

Cannings women probably went up to pick the little 'burnet berries' for a wine that continues to be made here and there in a downland village.

If Hentner makes no references to English sheep-bells it can only have been because they were so familiar to him in his own country that they failed to impress him. But they were (and of course still are) a most pleasing feature of every downland flock, and the air of Cannings and Bourton and Horton downs used to be musical with their chimes. Shepherds often owned their own peals and were as proud of them as George Ferebe of those in the church tower. In Devizes museum are some old sheep-bells of heavy durable metal from Bishops Cannings that may well have hung from the necks of seventeenth century sheep. But since such bells are difficult to date nothing can be said with certainty.

Cannings downs of course have always suffered from a lack of water. Only at their feet—under Easton, Bourton, Horton, and Roundway Downs do the springs ooze through the chalk to join the Salisbury and the Bristol Avon. But there were the dew-ponds. In Bishops Cannings parish, on a rough estimate, at least a dozen of these provided water for the sheep. Gangs of dew-pond makers moved about the county. A famous one lived at Imber. Another, who early in the nineteenth century still carried on a trade followed by their family generation after generation, was that of the Greens of Calstone. They may well have been responsible for some of the early Cannings ponds, as they certainly were for their upkeep later. An old farmer remembers how, when a boy, one of the Greens, 'a great big fellow with bushy side-whiskers'— came to repair his uncle's leaking pond on Bourton Down.

It will be remembered that it was in a dew-pond that the Moon-rakers are said to have fished for kegs of brandy dropped by smugglers.

Hentner probably saw his 'flocks extremely white' soon after their annual sheep-washing. The Coate and Horton sheep would have been taken to the Sheep Washing Close (referred to in the Court Book of 1659) not far from the old mill between Cannings and Horton. But those on the northern downs probably went to Calstone, just as they did till early in the present century.[12]

Shepherds

When George Ferebe climbed from the village to the downs he would constantly meet one of his 'silly shepherd swains', as he calls them in his 'Shepherds Song'. It is a pity he failed to enter in the registers the occupations of the parishioners whom he married and buried, as did Nathaniel Godwyn at the end of the century. There, in the space of about ten years, we meet with the names of fifteen shepherds—good Cannings names such as Dike, Drew, Minty and Hazel. Many of these may well be accounted descendants of Ferebe's shepherds, since their calling was one frequently handed on from father to son. There were Drews and Mintys and Dikes keeping their flocks on the downs when I was a child. In those days they wrapped themselves in great cloaks of navy blue cloth lined with scarlet that their fathers had brought home from the Crimean war—heavy, serviceable, much-treasured cloaks, worn till they fell to pieces. A carter thought his too precious to get wet and would roll it up when rain fell. Occasionally, when these cloaks were offered for sale in Devizes market, a crowd pressed eagerly round to buy them. Cloaks have always been an essential part of a shepherd's dress. Aubrey writes, 'Their habits, I believe (let there be a draught of their habit) is that of the Roman or Arcadian shepherds . . . a long white cloake with a very deep cape which comes half-way down their backs, made of the locks of sheep.' He goes on to lament that 'since 1671 they are grown so luxurious as to necklect their ancient warm and useful fashion,' and quotes from a contemporary pastoral, 'How lubber-like they lie upon the plaines.' Here is the perennial lament for the good old days.

George Ferebe's shepherds wore 'clod shoes' and 'pelt coates'. John Stephens the Younger, writing in Ferebe's time, says: 'His flock affords him his whole rayment, outside and linings, cloak and leather; and instead of much costly linnen his little garden yields him hemp enough to make his lockrun shirts, which doe preserve his body sweetend against court-itch and poxes.' For Stephens, as for writers in all ages, the shepherd represented the perfect type of man, sturdy, serene, devoted, living the ideal life. 'I cannot well resolve you,' he writes, 'whether his sheepe or he be more innocent. Give him fat lambs and faire weather and he knows no happiness beyond them. . . . His daily life is a delight-

ful worke whatsoever the work be; whether to mend his gar-
ments, cure a diseased sheep, instruct his dogge, or change
pastures.'

But in his enthusiasm Stephens forgets the driving snow and
rain and the boisterous winds from which, on Cannings downs
at all events, the shepherd had small chance of escape. Often there
was not even a furze or juniper bush to shelter him. He forgets
the deep mud about the fold; the purple, frosted hands; the long
cold nights at lambing time. But otherwise it is a true picture.
I shall always remember the innocent candid gaze of those Cannings shepherds, 'the simple faith that purified their souls'.

A figure whom the two Ferebes must often have met on their
rounds was the Common Shepherd, tending a flock belonging to
at least a dozen small owners, and thus differentiated from the
shepherds employed by the big landowners. Perhaps he was the
actual 'John Shephearde'[14] of the registers, who fathered eight
children during the first part of the seventeenth century. His was
a most important and responsible post. If for some reason he
could not be with the sheep himself, he must appoint a trust-
worthy substitute and on no account hand them over to the care
of children. He must keep a wary eye for wandering wool-pickers
seeking opportunity to rob the sheeps' backs. If he neglected a
sick animal or failed to rescue one from misadventure he must
compensate the owner from his wages, made up of appropriate
sums from all who shared his services. Some fifteen years after
George Ferebe's death certain Wiltshire magistrates fixed a maxi-
mum wage for shepherds tending not more than 600 sheep at
£3 6s. 8d. a year.[15] He must 'pitch and pen' the flock in orderly
manner, and see that crops suffered no damage.

Sometimes it appears that in the midst of the grazing grounds a
shepherd cultivated his own small garden where he perhaps grew
kale or roots for himself. Such a garden is shown on an old map
(dated 1770) in the heart of the downs north-west of Easton hill.[16]

The Downs

Of all places on the Cannings Downs the one that holds the
most important place in my story is Old Shepherd's Shore. For
here it was that on a June day in 1613, George Ferebe and his

parishioners entertained Queen Anne, wife of James I, as she returned from drinking the waters of Bath.

'Shore' derives from the old word 'sceard' or 'shard', meaning a cut or gap. Archdeacon Macdonald, vicar of Bishops Cannings for 50 years (1815-1862), tells us that in his own day 'the Shard' might often be heard on country lips. The gap in this case was a cutting through Wansdyke at the point where the old coaching road from Bath to London crosses it. 'New Shepherd's Shore', half a mile below, did not then exist; that portion of the present main road was still unmade.

Old Shepherd's Shore is marked now only by a few little weather-beaten trees, but when Queen Anne came driving along a little inn called The Shepherd's Rest probably stood there. Fred Minety, the oldest Cannings inhabitant, has told me how his father, born in 1819, heard tell of it as an ancient little place where beer used to be sold and where the lads gathered to play at 'chopsticks' on a raised platform east of the trees. A well is buried deep under the grass and a big housekey, of sixteenth or seventeenth century pattern, was found close by. Other far older objects lay undisturbed in Ferebe's time in the neighbouring barrows, including a fine little bronze soldier. A bronze brooch, thrown up by burrowing rabbits, was retrieved not long ago by a shepherd. Both are now in Devizes museum.

But many precious objects undoubtedly never reached safety. Such was a large golden ornament that in the 1890's a Cannings man, working for a famous Wiltshire archaeologist, uncovered with his spade. 'Ah,' he said to himself, 'that 'ud make three handsome brooches for my three daughters', and into brooches it was made. A less wary eye supervised diggers than nowadays and they themselves belonged to a different order.

Beside Old Shepherd's Shore lay, as I believe, the 'Shepherds' Bench Lawns' of the seventeenth century Court Books. What more natural than that here, in the very centre of the sheep grazing country, should be set a bench under a clump of trees where shepherds could rest and drink together before they separated to fold their flocks for the night? As they sat there it is likely that they looked down on a gallows, for here, close to the Shore, stretched Gallows Breach Lands[17]—a suitably lonely spot for a gibbet.

Only half a mile away to the north, close to the Roman Road and to four barrows, was a dew-pond which must have been in constant use. Even today a little water still lies in it, rushes grow, and an occasional wild duck comes to feed. Medieval people had a settlement near by, and its big rectangular outline is clearly visible. There, in the present century, were dug up bones of sheep, oxen, and dogs, as well as fragments of glass and pottery. If you feel inspired to walk the coaching road you will find Old Shepherd's Shore, 700 feet above sea level, a rewarding place from which to stand and stare before you start. Away to the east of you Wansdyke rears like a great dark wave as far as the eye can reach.

You at all events may know its extent and that it is post-Roman origin. But to those seventeenth century shepherds, sheltering in it from wind and rain, it was a mysterious and inexplicable affair —'made by the Devil on a Wednesday'.[18] On the eastern skyline is Roughridge Hill, where Prince Maurice and the Earl of Hertford drew up their Life Guards early on the morning of July 13, 1643, (after a very wet night) before the Battle of Roundway Down. That day the shepherds of Thomas Ferebe's time, with eyes accustomed to scan the heavens, saw 'the cloud like a lion rampant azure' that hung in the sky while the fight raged.[19]

But earlier in the century the shepherds' kingdom round the shore was a peaceful one, except for the fierce storms that have always swept it. Perhaps it was during such a storm that 'Nathaniel Webb of Rowde died at Shepherds' Shard' on a March day in 1748.[20]

All round still stretch the 'wild, wide houseless downs' of Ferebe's 'Shepherd's Song',[21] only now they are more cultivated, and one or two houses have appeared, including the little house with steep pitched roof at 'New Shepherds' Shore'. But still the wildness and wideness remain. The house just referred to was once known as 'The Shepherd's Shore Inn'[22] and probably was built in the second half of the eighteenth century at the same time as the new piece of road. Till the coming of Devizes waterworks late in the nineteenth century it was the only building between Beckhampton and the Roundway-Horton Cross Roads. Dickens' lovers identify it with the lonely inn where Tom Smart took refuge on a wild winter night, in the *Story Told by a Bagman*.[23] Structural alterations have taken place, but it still possesses 'a

wide and ancient staircase'. Some hundred years ago the licence
of the inn was withdrawn after a tragic accident.[24] Carters returning from Devizes market used to tie up their horses and stop for
refreshment. Unfortunately they often drank too freely and too
long till one day a restive horse broke loose and killed someone—
in all likelihood the Jacob Long who met his death, according to
the Parish Registers, 'with a road waggonnear' in 1809. Highway-
men found this lonely stretch of road excellent hunting ground.
Near Beckhampton enclosure an old track that served as a short
cut for travellers turning westwards from the Calne road provided
good cover. Beside this track once stood another gibbet where an
Avebury woman, who died in 1874 at the age of 103, remembered
seeing a corpse hanging. That same gibbet, or a similar one, probably stood there in the seventeenth century.

Between the fir plantation and the road a man shot for robbing
the coach lies buried. A stone used to mark the spot. Because of
widespread belief that not he but another was guilty of the crime,
gipsies passing that way to Tan Hill Fair would stop to lay a
tribute of flowers on his grave.

In George Ferebe's day, when life was more difficult for rogues
and vagabonds, Beckhampton ('Beckinton' in Ogilvie's *Britannia*)
was no doubt a less dangerous place. But even so people passing
that way would take pains to be away before dark. For not only
might robbers lie in wait for them but there were the fairies to be
considered. Aubrey tells of a countryman who, riding from Hack-
pen with a sack of corn, was 'led a pretty dance' from Beckhampton to Devizes. And at a spot not far away a shepherd vowed that
the ground opened under his feet and that he was taken 'into
strange places where he heard viols and other instruments of
music such as those played on by his master'.

In the latter half of the sixteenth century a little chapel dedicated to St Vincent, just beyond the Cannings boundary, was
falling into ruins, though it seems to have still been there in 1624,[25]
one of a multitude closed at the Reformation. When it stood empty
and desolate the people in the neighbourhood made their way
across the downs to worship either at Cannings or at Avebury.
Those who lived up there would clearly hear Cannings bells ringing on a Sunday morning when a south-west wind blew.

I have spoken of the inns at Old and New Shepherds' Shore.

George Skeate Ruddle's uncle told him that at the end of the eighteenth century another little inn stood at the northern end of the long fir plantation above West End, beside the old road already mentioned. It had disappeared long before the end of the nineteenth century but loose stones still lay about under the trees. At one time it would have been a halting place for men bringing wool to Devizes from the wide sheeplands near by.

In my childhood the old road, by this time no more than a sunken grass-grown lane leading to the plantation, was a favourite camping-place for gipsies. No sooner did the leaves begin to fall than they settled themselves down for the winter. A woman who died there in childbirth was called Gerania and I always thought she had been so named from the blue Crane's Bill that covered the banks of the lane. Later I learned that it was a favourite gipsy name. In the reigns of Elizabeth and James gipsies would seldom have been allowed even a temporary home in the parish.

Above this old road the downs rise steeply towards Roundway in terraces or lynchetts. Other even better defined lynchetts stand high against the sky on Bourton Down, and a successful seventeenth century vine-grower wrote: 'The hills by Cannings are proper for vineyards.'[26] They make a handsome pattern in green and white when the chalk strips have been newly ploughed, but it is exceedingly doubtful whether vines could ever have fruited in those windy uplands. For the Cannings downs can indeed be perishingly cold. People have died of exposure on them from time to time. Thomas Ferebe buried a 'strange youth found dead uppon our downes, the sheappard's sonne' on a January day, and 'three poore walkinge people' were brought down dead in the winter of 1597.

But when the weather was kind; when in summer a heat haze shimmered over the grass, and the colours of the downland flowers melted into one another; when innumerable sheep-bells broke the silence, and shepherds lay relaxed under juniper and gorse bushes, or played to themselves on rough pipes—then the downs must have been enchanting.

George Ferebe would find it no penance to visit his out-of-the-way parishioners in the morning or the cool of the day—to walk over the southern and eastern edges of Roundway and drop down to visit Griffin Nicholas at Nicholas Place, to take the air on

Easton Hill before calling on Thomas Sloper; to climb from Bourton Cross, pass through the gap in the hills to the north and join the shepherds on their bench outside the inn at Shepherd's Shore. Up here, where 'Cleanly Wynds the greene did sweepe', Ferebe might say with William Strode—

> Here would I sleepe, or read, or pray
> From early morn till flight of day :
> But harke! a sheepe-bell calls me upp,
> Like Oxford Colledge bells, to supp.[27]

When at Rogation-tide he beat the bounds of his parish with his choir, many other sturdy walkers would have joined him on his walk, and it may be that the girls wore in their bosoms 'tutties' (bunches) of one of the most typical of all downland blossoms, the little blue milkwort, or 'Procession Flower', whose white juices symbolized fruitfulness in women.

THE LOWLANDS

In the southern and eastern parts of Bishops Cannings the lowlands include many a marshy meadow. The basin of the young Salisbury Avon would have been marshier still 350 years ago, and far worse in 1010 when the Danes found themselves bogged down in 'Cannings Marsh' and could go no further.

After a wet autumn and winter the moisture stored in the chalk pushes its way through and bursts out at the foot of Easton, Bourton and Horton Downs into small triumphant streams that race along any available channel. Under Bourton Down the water makes its finest exit at Fishwater, birthplace of the Salisbury Avon. Here, where now is a tangled withy-bed, and a pumping-station (nicely planned, however) to steal away good Cannings water for Devizes, there used to be a series of small clear pools divided by narrow baulks, just visible between the giant leaves of butter-burr. At an earlier age this was known as 'Fishpond Ground', and here, by coincidence, lived for a time in the nineteenth century descendants of the ancient Cannings family of Vishlake or Fishlock. In those days all the village believed that this was the place where the monks from a small monastery, built on the site of Bourton

Manor, fished for their dinner. Sad to say no confirmation of this cherished tradition has been found, nor, I fear, ever will be, even though now and then something seems to strengthen it—as when I discovered on a map of Bourton dating from the late seventeenth or early eighteenth century in Devizes Museum that a field just north of Fishwater was called 'Prior's Furlong'. And always when I make an annual February pilgrimage to Bishops Cannings and enter the field still known as 'The Moor' beside the baby Avon (so named when Michael Tidcombe took his survey) I tighten my hold on the old belief. For here, under a thorn hedge raised well above the stream, grow luxuriant patches of green hellebore. And, as I stare down at its rich dark leaves, its emerald calyxes with their golden centres, I tell myself that once in this narrow field the monks tended their herb garden, and grew hellebore to purge people of 'flegme, choler, and . . . all melancholy humours', and to ease them when they were 'mad or furious, dull, heavy, or troubled by falling sickness', as Gerard affirmed it would do.

Old Squire Ruddle of my childhood put *his* faith partly in the fishponds and partly in his discovery that there had been a mill—a monastery mill, he made sure—in this same field. When draining work was being done about eighty years ago one of the men dug up a piece of curved oak, blackened by age and moisture, and carried it to his master.

'Bless my soul,' cried the squire, 'that's part of an old mill-head!' His nephew, who farmed Bourton till the beginning of 1959, had it carved into a tobacco jar. This same nephew reinforced his own belief in the monastery tradition by the discovery of a huge accumulation of oyster shells under the floor-boards of his dining-room. These, he concluded firmly, were the remains of the old monks' feasts.

But I must return to the Avon and the lowland meadows. The brisk unimpoverished little river was certainly turning the wheels of the mill in 'The Moor' when John Ernle was Squire of Bourton.[28] Gathering various small tributaries to itself as it goes, and crossing the line of the present Kennet and Avon Canal, it grew busy again a mile or so lower down at Nick's Mill. Nick's Mill stood just where the field path from Bishops Cannings joins the road through the Pewsey Vale at Horton. In Mill Mead[29] (the last meadow beside the path) the banks of the stream were deepened to prepare it for the task ahead. From the Parish Registers we know that this mill was working in 1714 when Jonathan Waterman buried the miller, John Dyke. Fred Minety's father heard tell of it when he was a boy. It may, indeed, have been the very same mill mentioned in a conveyance of Henry VIth's time.[30] and we can be pretty sure that when George Ferebe walked across the fields to Horton its wheel was turning busily.

Some time late in the eighteenth century Nick's Mill was pulled down and its place taken by another mill a few hundred yards to the north, close to the 'Sheep Washing Close'. I think that this was 'Shergold's Mill' mentioned in the Dean and Chapter Survey of 1800, since a mill-pond is also included. There used to be a large pond alive with moorhens above the present mill—the only one of its kind in the parish. Shergold was a good Cannings name throughout the seventeenth and eighteenth centuries. First they appear as 'Yeomen' then as 'gentlemen', and one of the family was curate in 1771. The red-brick mill, built on the same site, is of later date, but the old stone house beside it probably housed the Shergolds.

Here in my childhood lived Abel Hiscock, a relation of the Horton carpenter who designed the special plough for chalk soil mentioned by Hennell in 'Change on the Farm'. Abel, a fine broad-shouldered, whiskered old man, would stand no nonsense, no attempts by children to loiter beside his wheel. But sometimes when in the right mood he would allow a peep inside the mill. At his heels usually trotted his formidable pet sheep, Daisy, who loved to rush suddenly from some hiding place and knock people down. His wife had suffered more than once as she carried out the pig-meal. She herself preferred the sow, and let it stretch in comfort before the kitchen fire.

Now this mill, the last of the Cannings water mills (six are mentioned in Domesday), stands silent.

While on the subject of mills, mention should be made of two windmills in the parish. One stood on the high ground just south of the present Bridge Inn, called 'Windmill Ground', and the other on 'Windmill Knowl', a part of Roundway Down.

The Avon has led us to Horton ('the dirty town'), always an important part of Bishops Cannings. In the days when 'Cannings Marsh' defeated the Danes no doubt it lay deep in mud, but now the water meadows to the south of it are comparatively well-drained. They bore such pleasant names as Typettes, Cock Magget's mead, Fern Piece and Squirrels. Much of the land lies in the belt of upper greensand that spreads along the southern edge of the parish.

In George Ferebe's day Horton was evidently a prosperous place. Branches of the well-to-do yeomen families of Ruddle, Sloper and Western all lived here, and here too was the home of Simon Unwin, the biggest landowner. I have an idea that he—or his heirs—inhabited the oldest and most striking cottage block left in the parish. Now it is divided into two and is known as Townsend Cottages, but once clearly it was a single substantial farmhouse, a fitting home for such well-to-do people as the Unwins.[31] The excellent timberwork and the projecting leaded windows under their small tiled roofs call you to stop and look well, before you hurry on to Pewsey or Devizes. Inside the house are unusual beams, carved with a simple but effective pattern, the work of some local craftsman. Horton produced particularly good craftsmen. Not only did the Hiscocks live there, but also an interesting family called Ettry (or Itterie). In Ferebe's time John Ettry was a husbandman, but during the Commonwealth his descendants became carpenters, and then clock-makers. Edward Kite writes of them[32] as a race of men in the seventeenth and eighteenth centuries who, 'with meagre advantages in the way of education but with natural mechanical genius, built up and carried on for several generations a flourishing business'.

I have searched in vain for one of their grandfather clocks, though Mr Kite was able to cite two examples. The first, made in William III's time, was at Romsey, and the second belonged to a Trowbridge doctor. An amusing characteristic of the Ettrys was their fondness for the letter J in their choice of Christian names. John, Joel, Jerome, Jacob were repeated in each generation, and Joan and Jemima appear among their womenfolk. Joel, according to tradition, was not only a clockmaker but also a cunning astrologer. His Horton neighbours used to ask him to foretell the weather for them and to cast their children's nativities. Jerome Ettry, dying in 1797 aged 82, served as 'Lay Clerk' in the parish for 42 years.

Besides Townsend Cottages, a few early ones remain but most

have perished, including a whole row struck by lightning at the end of the last century.

Coate

Ferebe, going on from a visit to Simon Unwin or George Ruddle at Horton, to see parishioners at Coate (spelt usually 'Cote' or 'Coat' in his day) would use the little lane at the western end of the village, and if the mud was not too deep he might take the shady short-cut called the Drunge that branched off from it. Now it seems to have disappeared. Somewhere here stood an ancient oak where we always stopped to pick up acorns. This tree, so the old people of Horton affirmed, was haunted at dusk by the figure of a woman, who brought with her the scent of thyme.[33] From there Ferebe came on to Spaniel's (or more usually Spanell's) Bridge, and so into Coate itself. Coate, like Horton, was evidently a flourishing village in his day, though by the end of the nineteenth century it was a sad, tumbledown little place with over half the cottages in a wretched state of repair. Yet, set fortuitously between trees and high hedges, their deep thatched roofs green with moss sloping down to a few feet of the ground, they seemed to have grown into the landscape during their two or three hundred years of life. Some of them certainly existed early in the seventeenth century. Now most of them have given place to sanitary, well-built, but rather unloveable dwellings. However, one very old house remains—or at all events a portion of it, and that is the Manor Farm. The north wall is clearly part of the original house belonging to Thomas South when he farmed the Bishop's Manor in Coate in the early seventeenth century. Later the South family sold it to Walter Ernle of Etchilhampton.[34] In the modern bathroom remains an old door with clever hand-made hinges and small triangle carved in its upper edge to fit a notch in the door-frame—to keep it from rattling when the winds tore across the wide open meadows to the north. The name of another farm, Calcote or 'Cold-Cote', a quarter of a mile away, witnesses to the exposed character of this part of the parish.

These rushy, snipe-haunted meadows north-west of Coate must have been marshy indeed once upon a time, and even now nobody who wishes to walk dry-shod will venture in a wet season across them. In their midst are the little ragged copses still known as Laywoods (or Lea-woods) that appear so often in the Court Books of the seventeenth century. Here alders, ashes and oaks jostle each other for a place in the sun above the tangled undergrowth of water plantain, meadowsweet, and marestails that flourish in the oozy black mud. Today, as 300 years ago, Laywoods remain untamed and, I hope, untameable. The task of the villagers who owned strips in the surrounding fields, such as 'Fuddy mead' (or Floody mead), 'Miry Mead', and 'Andovers', was indeed a hard one. Sturdy though they were, their fortitude and that of their patient oxen must often have been sorely tried. Round about 1650 orders such as this frequently occur in the Court Books: 'That everyone having any way to their lands at Laywoods do carry the stones and repair Laywood Lane and cleanse the ditches adjoining the same . . . under penalty of 10d. to everyone offending.' And again : 'That everyone to whom it belongs do cleanse their ditches this side Fuddy Meade to a Place called Andovers.'

For here, in the little copses and the bogs round them, rise countless springs to feed 'Spanells' brook, a sluggish tributary of the Avon which travellers to or from Coate crossed by Laywood Bridge. (This affirms the Hommage, 'is in decay and ought to be repaired'.) Now the Kennet and Avon Canal sucks up some of the moisture and has its own Laywood Bridge.

Further west the land ceases to be water-logged and blossoms out (according to old maps) as Roses Mead. To the south of Laywoods a considerable bit of land was farmed by the stalwart Nash family, including a field where there grew legions of autumn crocuses, both mauve and white. Were they there 350 years ago to fill the hearts of children with the same delight as in the early twentieth century before they lamentably disappeared? And did the small-holders, returning from their strips in the evening, stop sometimes with spades and buckets to dig up the deep-set roots as a cure for their aches and pains?

Of the lane that leads back to Bishops Cannings itself I shall speak again when I come to 'Good Chandler'.

George Ferebe owned a piece of moist glebe on its eastern side, where marsh marigolds and ragged robins grew freely before it was drained. The names of two fields nearby still survive on the lips of old inhabitants—Bow Withy and Susannahs. Bowithy lies at the end of a little grass lane that used often on autumn evenings to be filled with smoke from gypsy fires. Susannah was a highly popular girl's name in Ferebe's day, and Hugh Gibbs, the village schoolmaster, so christened both of his daughters. Perhaps this field was called after them. A fine old timbered cottage stands at the head of the lane.

I have been speaking of the low-lying meadows in the east and south. North and west of Bishops Cannings rose the higher fields. There was the big common field called 'Towne Furlong'—'Tun-Vurlong' on the lips of old inhabitants today—that stretched right down from Cannings Hand Cross to the Bourton road. This piece of good dry land so near the village must have once been the scene of great activity. In 1647 the Hommage orders that every tenant shall make proper bounds at the end of his holding there. Beside the Town Furlong runs a smaller, narrower field called The Cratt, where men returning late from the inn at the end of last century declared that they sometimes saw a dark 'thing' slipping down towards them beside the hedge. One old man, catching a horrid glimpse of it, hid in the ditch for an hour or more and returned home cold and wet to an angry wife. No doubt from the time that an inn existed others suffered the same experience.

West of the church and of the Old Manor or 'Parsonage Farmhouse', the fields run gently upwards above a shallow valley watered by a tiny tributary of the Avon.

Most southerly of these fields was 'Prattes' (later 'Spratts'), a name which was going at all events as long ago as 1593,[35] the year of George Ferebe's arrival in Bishops Cannings. It is a big field and in those days was divided into Lower and Upper Pratts. Robert Bayley, the tenant, was ordered in June of that year to repair his house, but he took no notice and five months later was ordered to do so a second time. After three years the house remained unrepaired—perhaps because he was one of the Hommage who issued the order.

The footpath to Devizes used to cut across the middle of Spratts and continue through pleasant upland fields where larks always congregated more thickly than anywhere else. In the days when everyone used their legs freely it was a well-trodden path indeed, for it saved half a mile or more on a journey to the town. Under some giant elms in Spratts gypsies camped on their way to

Devizes Fair. A long row of black stockings hanging between the trees is stamped on my mind as a visible reproach to our own bare legs.

On the northern side of Spratts a small grass lane, unused now, led to the village Butts. The high field at the end is still so called, as also were a pair of ancient cottages till they were pulled down at the end of the last century. In one of them lived an old woman known as 'Sally Butts', who had Jimmy 'Wizzle' as her neighbour. ('His name was Merritt, but we always called him Wizzle, I don't know why,' said Fred Minety.) And in 1620 William Weston, then farming the Dean and Chapter Manor, was living at 'the Butts', and rented 'a close of meadows called 'Bryers'.[36] A flowering of soapwort, most domestic of plants, once marked the spot where the garden of William Weston, and later of Sally Butts, sloped gently to the stream. Another Butts lay beside the Harepath above Bourton, where it would have been easily accessible to Bourton and Easton men.

We travelled to Horton by way of the Avon. We return from it to Bishops Cannings by a path widely used in the past, but now lonely and overgrown. When the disused red-brick mill has been left behind a small gate leads into the lane once haunted by the ghostly sow. Innumerable feet trod it both in Ferebe's day and up to early in the present century. Sturdy Horton children walked daily along it to school. Among them in the first years of the fifteenth century, came little Robert Unwin to get the teaching that took him to Winchester in 1419.[37] Almost exactly 100 years later David Unwin followed in his footsteps. Friends and relations from either village used the lane; lovers, too engrossed to be troubled by old wives' tales, loitered there in the evenings.

Today, with the hazels cut low, the lane's air of mystery has gone and rank vegetation often makes it almost impassable. At its northern end runs the Kennet and Avon Canal, crossed by a swing-bridge. But Ferebe would have walked straight on into Broad Mead, and frequently have found the path under water. Even in my day we skated across it after a wet season, or rushed in a home-made ice-boat straight into the sunset. There must have been merry sliding parties on Broad Mead in the days when the drainage was even poorer.

West of Broad Mead a marshy field once known as Storks' Mead is marked unforgettably in my memory (before ever I knew its name) by my first sight of a heron standing motionless in the marsh. There is another Storks' Mead in the wet land under Easton Down. Many a Cannings man must have shot himself and his family a good dinner in those two fields. But the utmost caution was needed because of the severe penalties inflicted for shooting the Lord of the Manor's herons.

After Broad Mead the field path becomes a lane, incredibly muddy in winter. People treading it in those earlier days would be up to their knees. Of Snells, the field west of the lane, I shall say more later.

To the east lay the big common field of Charcroft, with a path to Bourton and Bourton Green running along its northern edge. Bourton is still well-peopled but Bourton Green scarcely exists. Yet once it was a flourishing little hamlet. Here, in a farmhouse of comfortable size, lived in Ferebe's day a branch of the ubiquitous Slopers. A box hedge still marks its garden boundaries. Clustered round it were eight cottages up till the last twenty years of the nineteenth century, and by a dozen or more a little earlier. All have gone. The last to survive stood beside a pond, gazing through its dark-lidded eyes at its own reflection in water continually rippled and splashed by a flock of white ducks. The pond remains, a little stagnant now, but a flock of ducks still enlivens it.

At the eastern end of the narrow lane that ran through Bourton Green, facing southwards across a wide meadow called Blackbirds, stand the two most ancient and beautiful cottages in Bishops Cannings. Careful study of old maps has led me to believe that once they formed a considerable farmhouse called Naish's Close, which may well have been the home of the Nash family in George and Thomas Ferebe's time. Of the Nashes and these cottages I shall have more to say.

The path from Bishops Cannings runs on across Blackbirds past the grounds of John Ernle's Manor house, and so brings us back where we started beside the young Avon and Fishwater. Ahead Easton Hill rounds off the line of downs that slope gently up to Tan Hill. Below lies the little hamlet of Easton, more populous once upon a time than now, and at its feet steals out a tiny winterbourne. Here in the seventeenth century stood two substantial farmhouses, in one of which lived Thomas Sloper, churchwarden and village patriarch. He must often have taken the field path to Bourton Manor to do business with John Ernle. But scarcely a soul uses it today.

NOTES TO CHAPTER IV

[1] *V.C.H.* VII. 189.

[2] His name disappears from the register after his marriage in 1611, for close on 200 years.

[3] Add. Charter. 37571. B.M.

[4] Court Book for 16th June. 37. Elizabeth, in the County Archives, Trowbridge. 'Lain is a Wiltshire word which probably denotes land . . . periodically allowed to lie fallow by being sown in irregular Laines or divisions.' (Wilts. Place-Names.)

[5] E. W. J. Kerridge, *Agriculture in Wiltshire in the Seventeenth Century.* To him I am indebted for much other information used in this chapter. Of the open field system in Wilts. in the seventeenth century he writes (in a letter to R. H. Tawney), 'It was quite common for there to be numerous common fields in a township—sometimes a score or more. These common fields, however, were merely typographical designations, i.e. the names were simply for the convenient identification of parts of common land, perhaps by marks of the compass, perhaps by landmarks of one sort or another.' R. H. Tawney himself writes to me that he believes that the motive for increasing the number of fields into which the common land was divided was in order to secure a freer hand in varying the common course of cultivation—whether the course was 2-field, 3-field, or 4-field.

[6] *V.C.H.* VII. 195. In the Court Book for Bishops Cannings, Oct. 17, 1646, when Robert Henley farmed both Bourton and Cannings, we read 'Michael Drew takes 9 acres of land called Rundway, to wit half of one acre in a place called the Cleeves, half of one acre in a place called Duck-Ruddle furlong, half of one acre in Shillands, and half an acre lying in Church Furlong and 2 roods lying above Amblecombe.' This Court Book, with others of the period, is in the possession of the Crown Commissioners.

[7] Q.S.G.R., ed. B. H. Cunnington, p. 25.

[8] The expectation of life *at birth* was roughly only 30 because of the very high rate of infant mortality.

[9] E. W. J. Kerridge.

[10] *The English Improver Improved.*

[11] E. W. J. Kerridge.

[12] ibid.

[13] See Chapter IX.

[14] In the All Cannings register the name 'Sheepman' is common in the seventeenth century.

[15] O.S.G.R., ed. B. H. Cunnington, p. 291.

[16] In the Library of the W.A.S. Devizes.

[17] Tithe Award Map, 1841.

[18] Aubrey, *Natural History of Wilts.*

[19] Rowde Parish Registers.

[20] Bishops Cannings Registers.

[21] *See Appendix C.*

[22] Map of 1770. County Records Office, Trowbridge.

[23] *Pickwick Papers*, Vol. 1.

[24] To Charles Wentworth of Uffington, whose grandfather was constable for Beckhampton early in the nineteenth century, I owe this and other information about this bit of country.

[25] In 1624 the chapel and its tithes were leased to William Dunch (Collections, Aubrey and Jackson).

[26] Sir W. Bassett of Claverdon is so quoted by Aubrey. MSS. of *Natural History of Wilts*. The Bodleian. A grandson of Sir Michael Ernle told Aubrey that he intended to plant a vineyard near his Etchilhampton home.

[27] 'On Westwall Downs' included in the Penguin Book of Eng. Verse.

[28] *V.C.H.* VII. 196.

[29] Court Book, 1659.

[30] *V.C.H.* VII. 196.

[31] A grant of the N. aisle in the church was made 'to ye family of the Unwins' in 1620—presumably for their tombs. See *W.A.M.* VI.

[32] 'Notes on Wilts Clockmakers,' Wilts. Tracts, 145. Series 241.

[33] *Vide* R. Coward, Letter to *Devizes Gazette*, 1896.

[34] *V.C.H.* VII. 190.

[35] Court Baron for Cannings Cannonicorum, June 16, 1593.

[36] ibid.

[37] *W.A.M.* VI. 131-32.

CHAPTER V

Church Life and the Churchwardens

CHURCH LIFE

IF George Ferebe was a conscientious parson there was plenty to keep him busy in his big scattered parish, though fortunately for him neither the chapelry of St James nor Chittoe, (usually 'Chittawe' in his day) five miles away as the crow flies, came directly under his care. But it was part of his duties to keep an eye on both, to appoint the curates in charge at St James, to sign the registers from time to time, and to maintain a fairly intimate relationship with the more important inhabitants—such as the Drews in Devizes, or the Nicholas family at Roundway.

As for Chittoe, his obligations seem to have consisted merely in the payment of 6s. 8d. a year to provide services in a little chapel that has long vanished.[1] Occasionally a Chittoe couple came to be married in the mother church, and later the dead—or some of them—were brought across the downs to be buried. A track called 'The Burying Road' leads off westward from the old road through the present fir plantation. George Ruddle, of Westend, who died at a great age towards the end of the nineteenth century, remembered when he was young seeing the coffins carried down to the village. The hedges, so he said, were expressly planted to shelter funeral processions at the end of their bleak upland journey. The bearers' task was indeed a hard one, and they were relieved at given stages on the way.

When these journeys started and how long they continued we don't know because Cannings vicars often gave no particulars about the people they buried. George Ferebe usually indicated which part of the parish they belonged to, but by no means always, and less frequently as the years went on.

As has been seen Ferebe's own financial position was a comfortable one,[2] but the poverty of the majority of his brother parsons was appalling at this time.

In 1585, less than ten years before he came to Cannings, Archbishop Whitgift declared that out of 9,000 benefices over half had the incomes of not more than £10 a year, and many less. Even the payment of tithes was uncertain, and, 'unless the parson kept on good terms with his people, the tithe barn might stand empty'.[3] They went about ragged and ill-shod, tilling their glebe, milking their cows, turning their children out early to work. For now they raised families—often large ones—on an income that provided smaller purchasing power than that of the celibate clergy of a few generations before. Moreover much of the enthusiasm aroused by the Reformation had spent itself, and though some parsons remained devout and high-minded in spite of hard conditions many grew slothful and lethargic. Some drank too freely, like the parson who returned drunk from Salisbury, kissed all the maidens awaiting him in church and gave them each a 'tuttye' (nosegay) instead of hearing them say their catechism.[4] Church life in the Salisbury diocese ran particularly low, and was not helped by the frequent change of bishop. One sick or tired old man after another arrived in Salisbury. Between the years 1615 to 1621 George Ferebe owed allegiance to no less than five. Henry Cotton, consecrated soon after he came to Cannings, was buried in the autumn of 1615 and succeeded by Robert Abbott, brother of the Archbishop. Ferebe must have met him when he held a Visitation at Devizes in 1616 and was provided with 'a sheepe and lambe for his sustenance'.[5] In spite of ill health Abbott worked hard to restore the Cathedral, to give sound religious instruction to his people, and to improve their lot generally. It was said of him that 'he exercised a bountiful and discriminating hospitality'. But less than three years after his consecration he died of a painful illness after much suffering.[6] His place was taken by an elderly Prebend from Canterbury, Martin Southeby, who held another visitation in Devizes in 1618.[7] Within a couple of years he too was dead, and Robert Townson, Dean of Westminster, father of fifteen children, became Bishop. Ten months later he died 'in a mean condition'[8] and was buried in the Abbey. But at last, with the appointment of John Davenant in 1621, began a happier era which, however, came too late for George Ferebe to see much of it.

Church Services

Music played an important part in village life in those happy days when all sorts of humble people enjoyed it on home-made instruments and often sang together in harmony. The church on Sundays would have been full of cheerful sound as everyone joined in the new and popular metrical versions of the Psalms. Though hymns were not much heard early in the century it is possible that the young vicar, go-ahead and straight from Oxford, introduced Miles Coverdale's *Goastly Psalmes and Spiritual Songs*,[11] and also trained his choir to sing such an old favourite as 'Jerusalem, my happy Home', with its twenty-six verses. But he died just too soon to use George Withers' *Hymns and Songs of the Church*. Bishops Cannings was of course fortunate in having an organ so early, and such a musical vicar.

The prayers—most of them the same as those we use today—would have been said, not intoned. As for the sermon, to judge from 'Life's Farewell' and from the custom of the day George Ferebe gave his people good measure. Incidentally, he certainly wore a surplice, for he was no puritan like Mr Zegwich across the downs at Ogbourne St Andrew, who was 'presented' in 1606 for refusing to do so.[12]

Baptisms

During the thirty years between September, 1593, and September, 1623, Ferebe and his curate christened some 550 children, an average of just over eighteen a year. As a progressive he would have followed the new fashion of sprinkling the babies brought to him instead of dipping them, bound tightly in swaddling clothes, in ice-cold water. When parsons in the Reformed Church began to marry and have children of their own the barbarity of this practice was brought home to them vividly. But even so infant mortality continued excessive in Bishops Cannings as elsewhere. Unlike his brother Thomas later on, George did not, when christening his own babies (or other particularly privileged ones such as the son of Robert Drew of Southbroom), enter the day and the hour of their birth, to help an astrologer later in 'casting a nativity'. After a christening or a churching there was always a feast, and John Stevens tells us that the Hostess at the Inn 'is sure to be rid of two or three dozen cakes and ale by gossiping neighbours' on these occasions.

Among the surnames of children whom George Ferebe christened (or people he buried or married) occur ones with such a pleasant country flavour as Southernwood, Sparrow, Haywarden, Silverthorne, Ivie, Fishlake, Pottle, Spickett, and Startupp. As for Christian names, John was the most popular, with Thomas very close, and William not far behind. Robert came next, then Richard. Nicholas, Ralph, and Hugh all appear now and then, also Charles and Edward. Peter was rare, perhaps because of the break with Rome. It is noticeable that when Ferebe had been vicar for some little time and had made a place for himself in the affection of his people his own name grew in favour. Mary easily led the way for girls—especially as the memory of Queen Mary grew dimmer—with Elizabeth, Joan, and Anne (or Annis) some way behind. Susanna (Susan too, but less frequent), Margery and Margaret, Alice (or Alce) and Bridget (sometimes Brudget) were other favourites. Rebecca and Christian occur several times. Praxie and Lyskin appear once, and Ancilla (a handmaiden) was the name that Ferebe chose for 'the daughter of an harlott'.

Weddings

George Ferebe, or his curate, married 157 couples. Well into the seventeenth century marriages were prohibited between Advent and the Epiphany, and again between Septuagesima or Easter. Though the mobility of Easter makes it hard to say how strictly Ferebe observed this practice it is clear from the registers for the fifteen years between 1608 (when separate entries begin regularly) and the autumn of 1623, that only one March wedding (and that on the 26th, which was probably Easter Monday) is recorded and no more than two or three in Advent.

While the inhabitants of the various parts of the parish intermarried freely, it was rare indeed to find anyone taking a 'foreigner' as husband or wife. Both Susan and Ann Ernle did, but their case was different. They moved in 'county' society. Otherwise Thomas Sloper, boldly going across Salisbury Plain to

Wallop for his bride; William Nash choosing Alice Rumming
from North Newnton; and an unknown Cannings girl marrying
Thomas Gurgenill of Calne, seem the only examples of such
marriages in George Ferebe's day.

Funerals

At this time the sensible custom prevailed of digging graves from
one end of the churchyard to another and then working back
again in the opposite direction. Thus encroachment on valuable
land was unnecessary, and space for the living was not sacrificed
to the dead. But as a result of this practice a great many old head-
stones have, of course, been lost, though a few seventeenth
ones are sunk deep in the grass.

Because the wool trade still flourished, 'burial in woollen' was
not yet obligatory and people could shroud their dead as they
chose. The Ernles paid fines for burying two of their family in
linen much later in the century.

Sunday and Lenten Observance

Since James I, by the proclamation issued soon after his arrival
in England, had shown that he had no wish to see the Scotch
Sabbath reproduced in his new kingdom, we may be sure that
Cannings men made their way to the Butts after church, or played
football down the lane or on the downs, or skittles at the inn.
Though in neighbouring places people got into trouble for bear
and bull-baiting and immoderate drinking on Sundays, or for fishing and playing bowls in church time, Cannings folk seem to have
offended less often.

Rules about the keeping of Lent were posted everywhere and
because there was much laxity over this the J.P.s of Wilts were
required to be specially careful in the example they set to others.[13]
The rule about eating fish was prompted as much by a desire to
bolster up the fish trade as to promote abstinence. Devizes, with
its important fish market, would feel a particular interest in this
matter, and in 1615 a fresh Proclamation ordering abstinence from
meat-eating was posted in the town. Only those with a special
licence from their pastors could eat meat in Lent. Such was the
case of Sarah Drew of Southbroom who obtained a licence from
Thomas Ferebe because she had been 'very dangerously sick since

the beginning of August last, and being not yet recovered of the same sickness but continuing weak and ill'.[14] Perhaps Sarah, still a girl in her 'teens, suffered from being the tenth of Robert Drew's eleven children.

The Churchwardens and their Duties

At the north-east end of the chancel of St Mary's Church is a handsome little vestry with vaulted roof and big open fireplace. A staircase so narrow that no fat man can climb it leads to a priest's chamber overhead. In this vestry the parish meeting, warmed by a good log fire, once a year appointed the new churchwardens. No one might refuse office by pleading that they were too busy, and many a newly-elected warden—usually a small yeoman farmer—must have trudged home with a heart heavy at the thought of what lay before him. To begin with he and his fellow-warden must attend to the fabric of the large and costly church, paying for it out of parish funds. This included, for Robert Nash and John Stevens in 1603, the weighty business of helping George Ferebe to hang all those new bells. From parish funds, too, they must pay the wages of the clerk and sexton, the expenses of Visitations, and for sundry other things. Under an injunction of Queen Elizabeth's time they must provide 'a comely and honest pulpit'; the strong alms-chest with three keys that still stands in the nave; 'the book of the whole Bible'; and a Register. The earliest one, of parchment, is inscribed on the first page, 'The Register Booke for Cannings Ep. wherein is all Christenings, Weddings and Burialls from the date here as foloweth, November 24th 1591. Richard Slop, Michael Pounde. Churchwardens.'[15]

They must look after the church's property in the parish—consisting of three acres in Horton Field and smaller pieces in Bourton and in 'The Sands', between Bishops Cannings and Coate—keep accounts (a heavy task for men of little learning, some of whom could only sign their name with a mark), impose church rates, and distrain the goods of those who refused to pay. On Sundays they must see that the able-bodied occupied the pews engraved with their names. Unless a churchwarden belonged to the type who enjoyed bringing a wrong-doer to book, the absence of any-one, or his repeated absence at all events, meant a tiresome inroad on a warden's time. For instance, if a man from the far end of Coate or one living on 'The Downde', at Harpits beyond Easton, or from some other outlying part of the parish was absent, there might be a tedious journey along a muddy track to collect a shilling fine, sometimes from a rude or angry man or woman. But perhaps in Cannings there were none like the innkeeper's wife across the downs at Calne who, reprimanded for non-attendance, answered tartly, that she 'must tarrie at home to keele the potte lest peradventure her porridge should rune over'.[16] Small blame to busy yeomen if they often turned a blind eye on empty pews. Even though one warden was usually resident in either Horton or Coate there was still much ground to cover. When parents failed to bring a baby to be christened within a month of birth that meant the collection of another fine. Nor did the churchwarden's duty end with church matters. Even more arduous were his civil responsibilities and those put on him in his ex-officio capacity as an overseer.

An an overseer, he must provide muskets and equipment for Cannings soldiers serving in trained bands, and relief both for their wives and themselves if they had been pressed into the Army. When Thomas Jones, carried off against his will to serve in Spain and Ireland, returned in 1611 to Bishops Cannings, the churchwardens put his claim to a pension before the magistrates, backed by a certificate from several of his neighbours. He got his money in the end through the intervention of Sir W. Waad who, from the Tower of London, looked after the rights of pressed and disabled soldiers.[17] And as overseers, the churchwardens must co-operate with the village constable to suppress drunkenness and collect a fine of 5s. from those who made a nuisance of themselves. Another was due from the innkeeper if he charged more than 3d. a gallon (in the early years of the seventeenth century) for his ale. Parents of illegitimate children were required to pay for their misdeeds. Such was Elizabeth Ducke with 'a daughter begotten in fornication' in 1591, and Robert Slop, himself a churchwarden's son. When more severe treatment than a fine was called for the warden handed the business over to the magistrates. In 1610 they sentenced a Devizes woman, mother of a bastard, to be 'whipped from the waste upwards, because she hath most unnaturally left her saide childe.[18] Fortunately in Ferebe's time bastards were rare. Only three are recorded between 1593-1623, whereas sometimes in the eighteenth century three times that number are recorded in half the time.

When wanderers came to the village the churchwardens must look after them. In 1596 John Woodruff and John Caswell had to see that 'a poore begar boye' was properly buried, and their successors next year were responsible for the 'three poore walkinge people' already referred to. On Thomas Cooke and Robert Dicks fell the duty of making 'George Knave', a 'poor wandringe man' bring his son to the church for baptism in 1593. Though they may not have insisted on the customary whipping, they and the constable were bound to see that George was sent back to his native place afterwards. It is amusing to find Thomas Ferebe christening one such wanderer 'Ulysses'.

These are only a part of the responsibilities that surrounded the churchwardens of Cannings. Small wonder if those elected at the annual vestry meeting felt no great elation even if, as sober god-fearing citizens, they accepted the office without fuss. However, to sweeten their lot, they, the parson, and other parish officers feasted together at the inn close by when the annual vestry meeting was over. Such a custom was kept up in the village till late in the nineteenth century. I wonder if George Ferebe and his wardens ever went blithely from the church only to find that someone had forgotten to order the dinner—as happened on one sad occasion in Victorian days?

Of individual churchwardens more will be said in the second part of this chapter.

SOME OF THE CHURCHWARDENS

Richard Snell, his Family, and Home

When I first met Richard Snell in the Parish Registers as one of George Ferebe's earliest wardens, and also noted that 'Snells' had once been a house 'of some pretensions',[19] my interest was at once aroused. The name seemed vaguely familiar, though for the life of me I could not say why.

Talk with the two oldest inhabitants of the village soon provided the clue. The first old man recalled to me something that I had forgotten—namely, that on the south side of the lane leading to the canal and Horton is a large field known as 'Snells'. 'Snails' the children used to call it. On its northern border runs a little stream so overgrown with willow herb and meadow sweet that you only know it is there by its small buried voice. When we were young it endeared itself to us by a jointed wooden doll fixed cunningly on a low platform, who forever bowed and straightened herself above the water. Not far from the gate into the field this brook widened into a pool where you saw the church spire clearly reflected when the cows from Court Farm had not recently churned it up. But now a tangled mass of bullrushes and reeds fills it.

'One day,' said my old man, 'I was mowing the grass down in Snells, close to the brook, when my scythe struck something hard, and there I found a great flat stone, a yard or more square, that looked as if it had been part of the foundations of a house some time or other.' My second old man (who is over eighty) remembered that when he was a little lad there were four deserted, tumble-down, stone cottages, all in one block, standing on this very spot.

It gave me a thrill of pleasure to know that here beside the pool had stood the home of the Snells, and particularly of Ferebe's churchwarden, Richard. Later, in a survey of the Manor of the Dean and Chapter dated 1800, I found 'Snell's Homestead and Orchard' and 'Snell's Ground'. Now that I knew just where the family lived, the next thing was to discover more about them. It seemed that the Snells had for a long period of years been Reeves to the Abbey of Glastonbury. Richard of Cannings' great-great-grandfather, another Richard, acted as bailiff for the monks' property at Kington St Michael in N. Wilts, birth-place of John Aubrey. According to tradition he feathered his nest in the same way as the unjust steward of the parable. He foresaw the Fall of the Monasteries and provided for the future by omitting to settle with the Abbot for arrears of rent. With this money he bought up the estate at the right moment, and in 1543 his son Nicholas was granted full rights to it.[20] Here he settled himself, bought a house from Aubrey's grandfather, and gave his children a comfortable start in life.

His eldest son, also named Nicholas, acquired land for himself at Horton (then called Horton Quarles) and in addition leased the manor of Cannings Cannonicorum from the Dean and Chapter.

ne held Courts in his own name.[21] In all likelihood he was living at Snells before his father's death, and very possibly built it himself with stones from the ruins of the bishops' house on the other side of the brook. In the county he became an important figure—represented it in Parliament and was Sheriff in 1565.

Horton Quarles he settled the year before his death in 1577 on his eldest son, John who evidently did not want to be bothered with land so far from Kington and it passed to two members of old Cannings families, Simon and Thomas Weston.[22] It is worth while to recall here that this same John was grandfather to Sir Charles Snell, of whom Aubrey writes in his *Brief Lives*. Sir Walter Raleigh, he tells us, loved in his youth to have as his companions 'boysterous blades . . . except otherwise uppon designe, to gett them engaged for him, e.g. Sir Charles Snell, of Kington St Michael in North Wilts, my good neighbour, an honest young gentle man but kept a perpetuall Sott. He engaged him to build a ship, the Angel Gabriel, for the Designe for Guiana'. But when Sir Walter was indicted for treason this honest young gentleman lost much property and also his lease of Bishops Cannings (which, as the eldest grandson of Nicholas Snell he still held from the Dean and Chapter).

Charles' father had a younger brother, Thomas, who acquired a house at Loxwell, in the south-west corner of the county, where, some 400 years previously a band of monks had tried to found a Cistercian monastery on land given them by Henry II, then Earl of Anjou. For three years they lived in wooden huts, suffered great hardships, failed in their task, and moved down to Stanley, on the banks of the Marden, where more trouble awaited them. Because of the marshes they could draw no water from the river. Valiantly they set to work and built, 'by the help of God and the Lord Jesus Christ and good John the Evangelist', an aqueduct to bring water from the spring at Loxwell.[23]

When Thomas Snell went to Loxwell remains of the aqueduct would still have been clearly visible.

Thomas, like his grandfather and his elder brother, was an important person—a J.P., a Captain of Lancers, and Sheriff in 1599.[24]

His oldest son was Richard, Ferebe's churchwarden, who, during his father's lifetime, made his home at Snells. Here his wife, Judith, gave birth to five children between 1596 and 1604—

Mary, Margaret, Nicholas, Richard and Annis. Nicholas lived only one day after his baptism in 1601, and Annis died when she was but six months. Of his other children, Richard certainly survived for we find him in the Visitation of Wilts. for 1623. John, the churchwarden's oldest son, was probably born at Bishops Cannings before the registers began.

When Thomas Snell died, Richard and Judith moved to the beautiful old house at Loxwell, pulled down only a few years ago. But still there was John to carry on the name of Snell in the parish—John with his Gloucestershire wife Katherine (née Pleddall or Pleydall) and his three children, Charles, Elizabeth, and Judith. In 1634 we find him signing the registers on behalf of one of the churchwardens, though he does not seem to have held office himself. So once again there were young Snells to roam the meadows round their home, and to go to church by the path across Court Close, over the site of Bishop Erghum's house.

After that entry the Snell family appear no more in the registers. The connection with Cannings must have been finally severed when Richard died and John succeeded him at Loxwell. But the name of the Snells' old home crops up again when William Nash, yeoman, is recorded as living there in the eighteenth century. Thus, from the day when Nicholas, Lord of the Manor and Sheriff of Wiltshire, inhabited Snells, it gradually declined till at last, divided into four cottages, it crumbled away.

From a worldly point of view Richard Snell's branch of the family also declined. No more sheriffs, magistrates or Captains of Lancers are found among them. Their estate, too, probably dwindled. But the strength of character that had built up their position in Wiltshire remained. In the latter half of the seventeenth century they are no longer props of Church and State. Instead we find them followers of George Fox, ready to suffer and if necessary die for their faith.

From Besse's *Sufferings of the Friends* we learn that Benjamin Snell (of Rowde) had six cows, a bullock, and £20 taken from him, because he attended a meeting at Bromham, and that Jonathan Snell (of Loxwell) lost goods worth £18 for a similar reason. Both Benjamin and Jonathan were almost certainly grandsons of Richard.

Finally real tragedy occurs. Jane (wife of Benjamin) was taking part in another meeting at Bromham in 1684, when in marched the Rector with two justices, arrested her, several other women (including Mary Martin of Bishops Cannings, a descendant of another early churchwarden of George Ferebe's) and two men. Because they refused to take the Oath of Allegiance, they were put in Devizes Bridewell and kept there for five weeks. An order for their release arrived too late to save Jane, who had fallen ill. We started off with the prosperous steward of Glastonbury Abbey, and end with a woman who died in prison for conscience sake.

The Nashes and 'Naish's Close'

As long as there have been trees in England there have been ashes, and in Bishops Cannings there have been Nashes as far back as the registers go, and no doubt long before.

In 1599 Robert Nash de Cannynges' signs the new register with George Ruddle of Horton—'who bought this book in their tyme' —and again in 1603. His sons, his grandson, and his great-grandson, follow him as churchwardens. The 'Jone and Chrystin' who had a double wedding in 1595 were probably his daughters. No less than 200 times does the family's name appear between the end of the sixteenth and eighteenth centuries.

Right up till the early eighteenth century they kept their status as yeoman farmers. Michael Nash, who was living in the old home of the Snells in 1768 is so entered, though a Horton branch have become 'labourers'.

How important the family was once upon a time is shown in the amount of land and property called after them. In the Dean and Chapter's survey for 1800 we find 'Nash's Homestead', close to 'Nash's Laywoods'; 'Nash's Moor and Coppice', 'Nash's East-mead', 'Upper Nash's Ground' all lying in the same south-west bit of the parish. Here, too, beside the Devizes road is the field once called 'Nash's', but 'Old Men's Land' in a map of 1841. An unknown Nash left this 'forever' to the two oldest men born in the tything of Cannings Cannonicorum. Because it is worth so much less than formerly, its annual rent of £8 now goes to only one old man, Fred Minety, who incidentally typifies all the vigour, pride and independence (though not the simplicity) of the true

Cannings' native. 'But that there land only comes to us when we're too old to work it,' says Fred.

Besides this Nash property round Lea Woods, in Bourton also stood a house called 'Naish's Close' and beside the little road that runs up to the Harepath and Bourton Down was 'Nash's Hill'. Here the last of the land-owning Nashes, John Nash, still owned two fields (one on the left side of the road, and another by the Harepath) at the end of the nineteenth century. He ran them as a market garden with Fred Minety, then a young lad, to help him. But latterly John preferred to sit snug at the inn while Fred and another boy dug and sowed and planted. When the old man died a bachelor, with no Nash to succeed him, the land passed into the hands of the Crown Commissioners. Apart from George Skeate Ruddle, John Nash was the last independent landowner in the whole of Bishops Cannings.

And what of 'Naish's Close'? Though the title has long been lost careful study of an old map[25] inclines me to believe that it may reasonably be identified with the two oldest cottages in Bishops Cannings, the pair that face southwards across Blackbirds at Bourton Green. Like many others they are anonymous now. So substantially are they built that they have outlasted all those other lost homes at the Green. Theirs are the thick walls and the massive timbers (with uprights firmly rooted in the ground) that are typical of the best of their kind. Inside they are spacious and comfortable. The eastern cottage shows the outline of a huge fireplace, nine feet across, surmounted by a beam still in perfect condition, though painted over and hidden behind a drop curtain. The western cottage possesses a living-room eighteen feet long, and a skilfully moulded beam that supports the ceiling from one end to the other. Here for a while the famous Cannings drum found a resting-place.

There was a time when this handsome pair formed one substantial farmhouse and it is here, between the water meadows and the high white lynchetts, that I like to place Robert Nashe de Cannynges, that sound and solid man, who was ready to take on only a year before his death the heavy responsibilities of a churchwarden; the man who handed on the office to generations of his successors, whose name still clings to the oldest parish charity.

'Nash's Homestead' and 'Nash's Hill' have vanished but Nash's

Close may still be a comfortable home in a hundred years' time, and though there are no Nashes left in Cannings their charity goes on 'forever'.

The Slopers or Slops and Their Home Under Easton Hill

Without the Slopers Bishops Cannings would have been the poorer both in the number and quality of its inhabitants. In just over 200 years (1591-1806) their names appear on 221 of the printed pages of the registers. Six young Slopers are baptized in one year alone by George Ferebe or his curate, and five times the family served him as Churchwardens. In so doing they were upholding an old tradition, for it may be remembered that a Thomas Sloper was one of the pair who signed the deed making over 'The Lady Bower' to John Ernle in 1563. This Thomas may well have been a son of Thomas Sloper, vicar of Cannings for 31 years in the first half of the sixteenth century.

Another Sloper, Richard, is warden in 1591 and signs for the first Parish Register. In 1597 and 1608 William Sloper de Eston holds office, and in 1614-15 Arthur of Horton also witnesses the deed of administration for George Ferebe's goods and chattels when he died intestate. So it continues through the centuries, till we come at last to Mark Sloper, Churchwarden in the mid-nineteenth century, a respected and widely known farmer throughout N. Wilts, 'than whom,' wrote Edward Coward, 'none rode straighter to hounds'.[26] Sometimes, especially in earlier days, the Slopers are plain 'Slop',[27] but this more primitive form disappears during the first quarter of the eighteenth century.

Slopers cannot be pinned down to any one part of the parish. They crop up everywhere. William, the thatcher, gives birth to twins at Westend. Others of the clan are found at Bourton Cross and Bourton Green, at 'The Downde', at Horton, Coate, and Roundway.[28] One of the earliest of all is Thomas of Knarstones. Since his daughter was baptized at Bishops Cannings it is likely that he lived on the extreme north-western edge of the parish and not down in Calstone itself.

Sometimes they are referred to as Gentlemen, and though an early Sloper disclaims the title at the Herald's Visitation of 1563, it occurs again in the next two centuries. There is, for instance, 'Mr William', father of over a dozen children, whom Avery

Thompson, the vicar, severely enters as 'Slop' after he has fathered a base-born son, christened Esau. But the most interesting of all the 'gentlemen' Slopers is Thomas of Easton, churchwarden to both the Ferebes. Michael Tidcombe's survey shows that he was a freeholder who farmed on a considerable scale. 'Thomas Sloper holdeth freely of the said manor 26 acres arable land; 8 acres of meadow, severall Downes for sheep, yearly rent 2s. and 6d.,' he writes. Today, a daughter of John Harraway still knows a piece of Thomas Sloper's holding, one of those long fields under Easton Down that take the curve of the hill, as 'Slopers' Ground'.

Born in 1562 Thomas lived for ninety-seven years, and remained active even in extreme old age. For when 88, he was required to view the highway at Bourton with two other yeomen in Whitsun week, 'and present the truth thereof'.[29] He shared, as far as a quiet countryman could, in the excitements of Elizabethan days, and would have been among those who welcomed Queen Anne at Shepherd's Shore. Thirty years later he heard the guns boom across Rounday Down. But for him, perhaps the most memorable day in his life was the 'Mondaie in Whitsun wek' (the spelling suggests this to be the curate's entry, not Ferebe's), in 1598 when he rode over Salisbury Plain to 'Wallope in Hampshire' to marry 'Joanne Tille', and bring her back from her river valley to the house called Townsends under Easton Hill. There she bore him many children —though nothing to equal the famous Harraway family, partly reared on exactly the same spot.

Before the red-brick Victorian house known as Easton Farm was built, the Harraways lived in the old thatched house that preceded it. But for a time, till their new house was ready, they moved into a second farmhouse that stood only 100 yards to the south. This was, I think, originally 'Townsends'—home of Thomas and later of William Sloper. According to old inhabitants it was a very ancient place indeed, and after the Harraway family had moved to their new home it remained empty except when a band of travelling Irish reapers came to help in harvest time and slept there. Its final destruction was commonly attributed to them, but actually was the work of John Harraway's old mother. She wearied of looking out day after day at so dilapidated a building and when the chance of getting rid of it safely came she seized it.

The reapers, their task done, had departed, leaving a fire smouldering in the grate. The old lady was at home alone.

Out she hurried and set fire to the thatch. The house, excessively vulnerable with its crumbling oak beams and its straw roof, went up in flames.

'Must have been those damned reapers,' said John when he returned.

'So it must,' agreed his mother.

'Still, 'tis a good riddance.'

'So it is,' she replied. But she was too pleased with her own part in the matter to keep her secret for ever.

A few stones lie buried under the ground where the Slopers' farm once stood, and some daffodils appear each spring to show that once there was a garden there.

The famous family to whom this resourceful old lady was grandmother numbered, for a short time, nineteen children—four girls and fifteen boys. So thick and fast they came that there were never enough beds or cots to contain them, and the old nurse slept with a baby in a drawer on either side of her. According to tradition, John said to his wife, 'Let's make it a score, my dear.' But Mrs. Harraway protested that she had done more than enough.

Yet never do I remember her with a hair out of place in her Queen Alexandra coiffure, nor without a colour in her cheeks that recalled the big sainfoin field under Easton Hill. Buoyant irrepressible kindliness and energy characterized her throughout her life. When she drove into Devizes on market days her cream-coloured pony was such a gentleman that she could relax completely and even fall asleep with the reins lying loosely in her lap. But with John it was a far different matter. He spun along at a terrific pace in his high dog-cart, though on the way home, after he had drunk hard at The Bear, the responsibility for his safe return also depended on the trustworthiness of his horse. When he and his wife turned their back on the green hill above their home and set out for Devizes market they were doing what Thomas and Joan Slop did all through the first half of the seventeenth century.

After fifty years with Thomas, Joan died on a November day in 1644 while the shadow of the Civil War hung over Cannings. Though the Battle of Roundway was over there was constant skirmishing in the neighbourhood, as the funeral of a soldier 'dyinge at Roundway' three days after Joan bears witness.

Fifteen years later Thomas joined her and innumerable other Slopers in Cannings churchyard. But he left a son, William, to carry on the farm. In the County Archives exists a Terrier of William's lands, including 'the house called Townsends in Easton', and the five-acre field still known as Rixons or Ruxons. This is also the name of a small right-of-way that runs southwards through moist meadows and makes a short cut to Horton. Gipsies were fond of using it in the Harraways' time, and one day John swore roundly at a woman for leaving a gate open. 'You're all jaw like an old sheep,' she screamed at him, 'and your head would be dear at a shilling!' What John replied is probably unprintable, for he had Irish blood in him and an extremely hot temper.

Old Thomas Sloper, in addition to William the heir, had another son christened Mark, born in George Ferebe's last year of life— the first of a long succession of Marks. The second one was buried in 1734, aged 84. On a buttress at the southern end of the church is an inscription to him adorned with a simple but pleasing design of flower and leaf. Mark, his grandson, fathered fifteen children— ten sons and five daughters—in rapid succession during the last years of the eighteenth century. Of these the second, yet another Mark, grew up to be the notable figure of whom I have already spoken—churchwarden to Archdeacon Macdonald, Trustee for Church lands, indefatigable rider to hounds. The old Sloper property at Easton had long since passed into other hands and he lived at Manor Farm.[30] Mark was a fine, upstanding man, with a large nose. At one of those old genial market dinners at The Bear, high-light in a farmers' week, a friend opposite drew his attention to a bit of cabbage that had lodged itself on this nose. 'You take it off then, neighbour,' said Mark, 'for 'tis nearer you than to me.'

It was an old Farmer Sloper, living in Blackwell Farm, who unwittingly warmed his lamb too well in the oven.

Now there are no Slopers to farm Cannings land, to live long peaceful busy lives, to bear immense families, to act as churchwardens, and generally to add richness and flavour to village life.

*The Ruddles—the Last Independent Landowners in Bishops
Cannings*

The sturdy yeoman family of Ruddles, who take their name from
the ruddle once so important in a sheep country, were only a
little behind the Slopers in populating Bishops Cannings. Later
they spread themselves into South Wilts. From 1591 onwards a
close succession of Ruddles are being baptized, married, buried.
They were prosperous yeomen who seem to have maintained their
position generation after generation. At least two pieces of land
formerly bore their name—'Ruddles' Piece', in the neighbourhood
of Easton, and Duck Ruddles at Roundway.[31] Early in the seventeenth century a Ruddle daughter married a Skeate (or Skate) and
from their seven children sprang another large Cannings' family.
Later on the two names were linked again by a second marriage
and have remained so.

Like the Slopers, Ruddles crop up all over the parish and serve
constantly as churchwardens. John 'of Eston' held office in 1598
and again eight years later. He could write his own name, but
not so some other Ruddles who followed him. Thomas Sloper,
the patriarch, was a near neighbour, but John, who died in 1612,
belonged to a much earlier generation. Another John was twice
churchwarden for Ferebe. George Ruddle, described sometimes
as 'de Horton' and sometimes 'of 5 acres' was probably the most
substantial member of the family. He was co-warden with Robert
Nash in 1599, and bought the stout leather-bound register book
with him that year.

Some tragedy attaches to his son and heir, Thomas. Thomas
died in 1637. Within two days his wife followed him, and within
six weeks two daughters, one of whom was only seventeen. Now
1637 was the year when Tan Hill Fair was banned because of
plague in Devizes, and it looks much as though the Ruddle family
was among the victims. The number of deaths in Cannings was
unusually high for the last months of 1636 (with the year ending
then on March 25th) and throughout 1637.

Among George of 5-acres' many nephews was another George.
History repeated itself when in the late nineteenth century there
sat in church on Sunday mornings, in the front pew, old George
Ruddle 'the Squire', and his nephew 'young George'—'Old George'

with bald head and side-whiskers and ancient broad-cloth coat, and 'Young George' always smart and well groomed. On week-days he often rode twenty miles to a Meet, or drove along the roads in a high yellow dog-cart drawn by the fastest horse he could buy. When his uncle died he succeeded him as squire of the Manor of Bourton, farmed much the same land as the Ernles, and lived in the same house. He was an inveterate and unrepentant cock-fighter who managed for years to elude the police. Some-times the sport took place in a remote barn beside Wansdyke, sometimes in the garden, sometimes on the parlour carpet, and even—or so it was rumoured—in a pit made by lifting the dining-room floorboards. A first-rate intelligence system was maintained by the gift of slaughtered birds to neighbouring cottagers, who consequently were always ready to bring news of approaching police. But at last he was caught and fined £100.

A silver salver, presented on the occasion by his friends and collaborators and engraved with their names, was one of his proudest possessions.

In extreme old age he was a gentle, patient old man who sat in his wainscotted room crippled with gout, while handsome little game-cocks looked in at him through the windows and tapped on the panes for food—unaware of the bloody fate of innumerable ancestors. Perhaps John Ernle, unperturbed by fear of the law, indulged in the same sport 300 years earlier.

George Ruddle died at the end of the bitter spell in the winter of 1959 and was laid in the family tomb. He was the last of a race who peopled the parish for at least four centuries, and the only independent landlord in Bishops Cannings. But it is pleasant to record that a nephew, whose mother was a Ruddle, succeeds him.

Robert Nicholas and the Nicholas Family

Robert Nicholas of Coate was churchwarden in 1602. We know no more of him except that George Ferebe baptized four of his children, that he and his son Thomas retained the title of 'gentle-man', and that Sir Oliver Nicholas, cup-bearer to James I, belonged to the same branch of the family. Gradually, however, its status declined, till 100 years later we find a descendant of the Coate Nicholases working as a blacksmith.

Over at Roundway, however, lived Robert's far more important cousins. They and their ancestors had been there since 1300, and perhaps even earlier. One of them had the unhappy distinction of being 'slain without the gatehouse' in the fifteenth century.[32] The site of their ancient home, Nicholas Place, was traced with care by Edward Coward, who farmed the land in Victorian and Edwardian days and was a keen local historian. Nicholas Place he set in what is now known as Autumn Crocus Field, lying close under the steep down, at the end of Quakers' Walk. Here the unmistakeable signs of a house of considerable size[33] can still be clearly seen.

About three years before George Ferebe came to Bishops Cannings, Maria, eldest daughter of Thomas Cook, his first churchwarden and Steward to the Bishop of Salisbury, must have given her father much satisfaction when she married John Nicholas of Roundway, and since her new home was only a couple of miles away, she was still within easy reach. Even when she and her husband moved to Devizes, to the old house now called 'Hazelands' in New Park Street, she was still not far away. Babies kept her busy; she bore seven in the next twelve years. Moreover she and John were under covenant to give John's father, Robert, board and lodging whenever he wanted it.[34] Of her seven children, one became famous—Judge Robert, Recorder of Devizes, stern and ardent Parliamentarian, harshest of Archbishop Laud's judges, an unloved and perhaps rather unloveable man. When he died (at Seend in 1677) and was buried at his own wish 'in the sepulchre of my ancestors within the Chapel of St James, in the parish of Bishops Cannings', neither his relatives nor the townsfolk put up any memorial to him.

Of different sympathies was another member of the Nicholas family, namely Sir Edward, Secretary of State for both the Charles. He heartened Charles I in his most difficult days, and helped to plan—though against his own better judgement—the flight to Scotland. To Charles II he showed the same loyalty, and he reduced himself to extreme poverty abroad on the King's behalf. Since he owned land in Bishops Cannings it is likely that Thomas Ferebe, if not George, met him from time to time.

Another Nicholas whom both of them knew well was John's brother Griffin who also lived at Roundway. Thomas Ferebe was on intimate terms with him, and Griffin chose him as a fellow

executor with Robert Drew of Southbroom. 'My lovinge friends'
he calls them in his will, and leaves them 'for their pains twenty
shillings apiece to buy them rings withal'.[35] Among Griffin's bene-
ficiaries was his niece, Eleanor, daughter of John and Mary and
wife of Marmaduke Byrd, a Devizes doctor. She and her husband
receive the interest on £120 (£12 a year) as long as she lives, but
if she dies and leaves no children the 'said Marmaduke shall have
no interest, title or right, or intermeddling whatever, of, unto, or
with the said £120'.

The Withers and Their Persecution

In 1607-08 Thomas Withers was a churchwarden. The name re-
curs with great frequency during the ministry of both George and
Thomas Ferebe, and indeed right on into the early years of the
nineteenth century. All over the parish members of the Withers'
family married, begat children, were laid to rest under the tall
spire.

But if you turn over the pages of the printed registers you find
that not all were buried there. Certain entries for the years 1678-
81 catch your eye.

'Marie Withers, widow, buried near the Gallows' Ditch within
this parish,' 'the wife of Ralph Withers,' and three other women
(one of whom, at least, was a Withers)—all are taken to this
strange-sounding place. Why? you may wonder, if you know no
more of the family history. The first part of the answer is that the
Gallows' Ditch was the old town ditch of Devizes, swallowed up
now by the Hillworth road, and that near it is the little burial
ground of the Friends. It lies in a quiet shady corner of the town
gardens, railed off from the gay flower-beds, the wide lawns, the
tennis courts. And the second part of the answer is that Marie
and her sister-in-law (Grace) were the wives of two Cannings men
who suffered long and bitterly for their faith.

We started off with Thomas the Churchwarden. He was one of
five brothers, a respected and prosperous yeoman, a staunch
churchman, performing the manifold duties required of him, including the fining of people who stayed away from church without good reason. But a month after his own death in 1624 the
wife of a Leicestershire weaver gave birth to a baby destined to
disturb profoundly the lives of Thomas' descendants. No longer

could they plough and sow their holdings peacefully in Bourton and Horton, no longer worship in the church of their fathers and listen to sermons from Thomas Ettwell, successor to Thomas Ferebe.

George Fox, after his wanderings in solitary places, his lonely night sessions in hollow trees, had received his summons, and henceforth knew no rest till he passed it on to others.. A year before he was born Thomas the Churchwarden had a grandson also called Thomas—'Thomas the Quaker'.[36] In his earlier, unregenerate days, this Thomas seems to have been a pugnacious person, in trouble with the manorial Court, disputing a right of way and digging up and stopping a footpath. [37] After George Fox's preaching had taken deep hold of him he showed the same obstinacy, the same determination, only this time it was in pursuit of his faith. When called on to make good before the Manorial Court his claim to 'one messuage and five cotsots of land, and two pieces of land . . . in Downacre and Waleron, and also ten acres of arable land called Boardland,[38] he refused to take the oath, and Marie, his wife, was examined instead of him. Robert Henley, Lord of the Manor, seems to have been unwilling to press a respected tenant too hard. But Wiltshire magistrates showed far less tolerance. After Thomas had attended a Sunday morning meeting at Market Lavington, he was seized, dragged into an alehouse (which in itself would be abhorrent to him) and condemned to a long period of imprisonment.[39] Later he was fined for refusing to take off his hat in Court. When his persecution was at its height, he, with other fellow sufferers, sent a moving petition to Judge Wyndham and the Salisbury Justices.[40] 'Wee suppose,' they pleaded, 'its not unknown how many and how great are . . . the troubles of us who are called Quakers which ever since wee were a People have beene inflicted and are yett likely, if the Lord open not people's hearts, to be continued against us.' The petition draws attention to the injustices heaped on them, and speaks of 'the sighes and teares which our long bondage have produced'. At the end comes an entreaty, 'Lett not our words and desires returne in vaine but favour us so much as to answer our complainte which we hope and believe will not be forgotten in the records of heaven.'

But the sighs and tears went on: the words returned in vain.

Worn out with imprisonment and ill-treatment Thomas died four years later (in 1669), when only forty-six. Perhaps the small plot beside the Gallows' Ditch had not yet been acquired, since he was buried in Cannings churchyard.

He would have been proud to know that his son, another Thomas, followed in his footsteps, though the going was never quite so hard as his own. But, like his father, Thomas refused all compromise with conscience. Called on to swear his fealty to John Methuen, now Lord of the Manor, he 'say'd these English words, "He could not swear." Therefore he was not admitted to his land.'[41] All the same he died in possession of it and of a cottage and close called Yonder Cotty, at Westend. John Methuen, like Robert Henley, was unwilling to coerce an honest man whose family was as much a part of Cannings as the land itself.[42]

Ralph, his uncle, suffered more than any other member of the Withers family. We find the Mayor of Marlborough—'a man of fiery spirit'[43]—indicting him as a common vagabond and flinging him into prison; we find him spending weeks in Devizes gaol in the company of common felons; having his clothes stolen by the bailiff; driven from a meeting at Marden by a 'venomous' vicar and his party, all armed with pikes, and again arrested; excommunicated because he had refused to be married according to the rites of the Church of England.

But before he died Ralph and other Cannings Friends were much heartened when William Penn addressed a big gathering 'in the Great Market Hall at Devizes . . . wonderful sober the people were, of all sorts', says Penn in a letter to Friends in Pennsylvania,[44] 'and greatly satisfied'. Probably, too, Ralph listened soon afterwards to a far more eloquent preacher, namely George Fox himself, when he spoke to 'glorious and powerful' meetings at the Great Fair at Bristol.[45]

Finally Ralph was chosen to go with another delegate to London in 1678 to back up Penn's petition that in future a Quaker's word might be accepted as a proof of loyalty. It seems likely that he died not long afterwards (since his name disappears from accounts of the Friends' activities), and that he was buried beside his wife near the Gallows' Ditch.

The sufferings of the Friends were almost over. Under James II other Withers, who were also followers of George Fox and many like them in Wiltshire, were gradually left in peace, till with the coming of William and Mary they were given full freedom to worship how and where they pleased. Sunday morning would have seen a small band setting calmly off by the footpath through Prattes and the upland fields, to join their fellow Friends at the little Meeting House in Devizes, for which the Withers were probably largely responsible.

The Stevens and Their Dick Whittington

The Stevens (or Stephens) were yet another sturdy, prolific family who shouldered at times the burden of churchwardenship.

One of them—William, who served with Richard Snell in 1595 —was the father, or so it seems pretty certain, of the Cannings Dick Whittington.[46] In 1622, when the boy would have been fourteen he was taken, perhaps on foot, perhaps by carrier's cart, to Bristol and there apprenticed to a grocer and his wife named James and Anne Gough. This couple owned a flourishing business on Old Bristol Bridge, crowded in those days with shops and houses. After eight years of diligent, faithful service Thomas became a freeman of the city (March 15, 1630).[47]

It seems that he, again like Whittington, married his employers' daughter, Anna, and that she too brought him wealth in the shape of the house and business on the Bridge.

Remembering his own fortunate start in life he took a young nephew, John Stevens from Bishops Cannings, into his home as an apprentice.[48] This was in 1646.

Though Anna bore her husband several children they all died young, and she also died at some date before 1654, when other apprentices were taken by Thomas. She was succeeded by a second wife named Cicely. By 1660 Thomas had so risen in the world that he was chosen as Sheriff, but he shrank from the honour and paid a fine of £200 rather than serve. Next year, however, he overcame his unwillingness, assumed the office, and later became Mayor of Bristol (1668).[49]

He died in 1679, a wealthy and important man. At his own wish he was buried beside his first wife and his children in the churchyard at St Nicholas, 'in a manner suitable to my degree and quality and according to the course and usage in Bristoll.'[50]

He chose Thomas Cary, minister of St Phillip and St Jacob (in which parish he had lived) to preach his funeral sermon in 'a 'plaine black mourning gown' to be given him for the purpose, plus a payment of £5, and a gift of twenty shillings as token of the love Thomas bore him.

The Will is immensely long and contains innumerable bequests to relatives, friends, and servants. His 'dear wife Cecill' was to manage his estates and to receive ample money and property; also 'the scabbard that was given me at the time of my mayorality'. Generous provision was made for all his servants, especially for Richard Joliafe, who was appointed an executor and was to have, in addition to an annuity, all of his master's wearing apparel not wanted by Jacob Selfe, Thomas' brother-in-law. Thomas particularly bequeaths Jacob his 'velvet dresse'.

Two-thirds of the property 'in and about the Bridge of Avon' goes to his Cannings kinsman, Robert Stevens, and the other third to Paul Weston, husband of Thomas' niece, Elizabeth, a descendant of the two Westons who farmed the Dean and Chapter's Manor in Ferebe's day.

All this shows how dear to him was his Cannings connection— further exemplified by his bequest of '£10 in money to be paid . . . into the hands of the minister and churchwardens and overseers of the poore of the parish of Bishops Cannings . . . to be and remaine as a store forever . . . and the profit thereof to be yearly distributed to the poore and sicke'. Thus Thomas, the prosperous, respected citizen of Bristol, clearly looked back and remembered his early days in Bishops Cannings and the hardships suffered by the old and infirm. This gift of his was augmented by £20 from Paul Weston for the purchase of bread on St Paul's Day.

Nothing of the two charities now remains, which is a pity, because they kept alive the name of an adventurous Cannings boy.

NOTES TO CHAPTER V

Church Life
[1] Rev. J. E. Jackson, *Ancient Chapels in Wilts. W.A.M.* XLI. 107. Chittoe ceased to be part of Bishops Cannings in 1845 when a new church was built.

[2] An agreement made in 1800 between the Dean and Chapter and the lessee of their manor commits him to 'yielding and paying yearly twelve

quarters of good, sweet and well winnowed wheat, sixteen quarters of good, sweet and well winnowed barley, to be paid and delivered to the vicar of the said parish church of Cannings at or in the Parsonage House of Cannings aforesaid at the four most usual feasts or days of payment in the year (that is to say, the Feast of the Nativity of John the Baptist, St Michael the Archangel, St Thomas the Apostle and the Annunciation of the Blessed Virgin Mary) by even and equal portions.' In the Wilts Archives at Trowbridge. A similar agreement would have existed in 1600. See p. 37, n. 16.

[3] Davis, *History of England*.

[4] Walker, *Sufferings of the Clergy*.

[5] Devizes Chamberlain's Accounts.

[6] *D.N.B.*

[7] 'Sugar and a wether' at a cost of 18s. 6d. were provided on this occasion. Chamberlain's Accounts.

[8] *D.N.B.*

[9] Ashley signs for the new register in 1601. He married a Cannings girl in 1599 and had four children. Later he seems to have resigned his curacy and to have become a churchwarden.

[10] *Vide* letter to Thomas Ferebe by Richard Berkeley in 1626. Q.S.G.R. Ed. B. H. Cunnington.

[11] A single copy remains in Queen's College Library, Oxford. *Vide* C. S. Phillips, *The Singing Church*. To him I owe other information about church music at this date.

[12] *Q.S.G.R.*, Ed. B. H. Cunnington, p. 14.

[13] ibid. p. 42.

[14] St James Parish Registers, 1634.

[15] Ten years later a second one also of parchment and bound in strong leather is signed for by Edward Ashley.

[16] *Q.S.G.R.*, ed. B. H. Cunnington, p. 35.

[17] ibid, p. 33.

[18] ibid.

[19] The Registers of Bishops Cannings, ed. J. H. Parry.

[20] *W.A.M.* IV. Rev. J. E. Jackson.

[21] Court Roll of John Ernle, Oct. 19, Eliz. IV. at Whetham.

[22] *V.C.H.* VII. 191.

[23] The story is told by T. Bowles in *History of Bremhill*, W.A.M. X.

[24] Thomas Snell's name occurs in an agreement of 1608 between the Deputy Lieutenant of Wilts. and the J.P.s, wherein he is asked to raise men and armour for the 'musters' in the Marlborough area. He is also among the Wilts. gentlemen who unwillingly disbursed £20 apiece to James I. (*W.A.M.* I and III).

[25] Tithe Award Map of 1841, also map of 1858, in possession of the Crown Commissioners.

[26] *W.A.M.* XLV.

[27] i.e. makers of the wide bags or breeches common even in Chaucer's day.

[28] An inventory of the goods of John Sloper of Roundway in 1643 shows that his house consisted of 'Hall, 2 chambers, a little chamber,' kitchen, buttery and scullery, and 5 bedsteads and bedding. Also the lease of a house in Devizes and for lands in Cannings Ep. and of 'a copyhold in Rundway'.

[29] Court Book for 1650.

[30] Built by Thomas Estcourt, then Lord of the Manor, as a hunting-box in the late eighteenth century.

[31] From the Court Book of 1647. 'And this same day came John Dogrell and took . . . 9 acres of land in Roundway, to wit, half of one acre in a place called Duck Ruddles.'

[32] *V.C.H.* VII. 191.

[33] Edward Coward. Notes on Roundway. Wilts. Tracts 146, series 241.

[34] Add. Charter. 37554. 40. Eliz. B.M.

[35] The Will of Griffin Nicholas. M.S. 34008. B.M.

[36] William Withers of Horton also had a son called Thomas, but the Court Books make it clear that 'Thomas the Quaker' farmed land in Bourton.

[37] Court Book for 1646.

[38] Court Book for 1658.

[39] Besse, *Sufferings of the Friends*, to which I owe other information about the Withers.

[40] *Q.S.G.R.*, ed. B. H. Cunnington, p. 244.

[41] Court Book for 1681.

[42] Waylen, in his *History of Devizes*, speaks of the disinheritance of the Withers, but in the Court Books we find them claiming and receiving back their land up to 1700.

[43] This same mayor sent another Withers to prison for 'singing of ballets contrary to the Statute'—probably religious songs. *Q.S.G.R.*, p. 230.

[44] Hull, *Life of Penn*.

[45] G. Fox, *Journal*.

[46] The only Stevens baby whose date of birth (1609) and name of father—William—fits in with the facts of his apprenticeship as recorded in the Bristol Archives—was originally christened William. The likelihood is that later he assumed the name of Thomas.

[47,48] Bristol Archives. Apprentice Rolls. Those taking up freedom on completion of apprenticeship were usually 21 years of age.

[49] Beavan. Bristol Lists.

[50] The Will of Thomas Stevens.

CHAPTER VI

Houses and People

A T the end of the sixteenth century and during the first part of the seventeenth a great many houses were being put up all over the country. Yet in spite of this building activity there remained a serious shortage, made more acute by the regulations requiring four acres of land to each house. Yeomen farmers were particularly unwilling to give up so much ground and later the trouble was enhanced by the disturbances caused by the Civil War in Wiltshire. An amusing yet pathetic seventeenth century petition sent to the magistrates by an old couple near Malmesbury illustrates this. It tells how the churchwardens and overseers had flung them out of their home and found them no other, so that they were forced to live in a hollow tree in the village street, 'to the great hazard of their lives, they being ancient people'.[1]

The churchwardens and overseers were responsible for putting up houses for the poor on the commons or waste lands—little wooden houses thatched with straw, costing about £3 apiece. But the other villagers often indignantly pulled or burned them down.

The Earl of Hertford, from his Manor of Burbage, some twelve miles east of Cannings, in a petition to James I, complains that when he enclosed a small piece of land and built a little house for one of his servants, three commoners, including a woman, 'came armed with long pike staves, daggers, bills and other weapons, did with great fury pull down a part of the house'. Interrupted by bailiffs, 'they returned later, completed the work with force and violence and carried away all the timbers and doors. . . . They did further grub up the apple trees and quickset hedges of the enclosed piece of ground'.[2]

Truly, between indignant commoners and reluctant landlords, the lot of the houseless was hard. In Cannings, with a rising population, there is a likelihood that house-hunger also prevailed but there are no records of similar rebellion.

As is the case of so many villages the face of Bishops Cannings has greatly changed during the last eighty years, and many are the ancient cottages that have disappeared. Now only a gooseberry bush, a bit of box hedge, a few daffodils, or a name on an old map, bear witness to their previous existence.

BISHOP ERGHUM'S HOUSE

There was once a house in Bishops Cannings of peculiar interest. As children we sometimes crossed from the south-east corner of the churchyard into a small moist meadow called Court Close (or just The Close) on the other side of the ditch, and climbed about the banks that rose rather unexpectedly within it. Here, we were told, in this bumpy little field had once stood a Bishop's house, and the banks indicated its foundations.

It was many years later before I looked further into this surprising statement. Erghum, the Bishop in question, had, it appeared, been Bishop of Salisbury from 1376 to 1388, and, because of his large manor of Cannings Cannonicorum he had either inherited or built himself a house there. Perhaps it was because of all the fighting he had seen in Flanders before he came to Wiltshire that he sought and obtained permission from the king to crenelate it.[3] Archdeacon Macdonald remarked that he must have been a timid man, since he made a similar request for his house at Potterne and later fortified his palace at Wells.

The Bishop's house in Court Close must have been in ruins when George Ferebe arrived in Bishops Cannings, but probably its position was still clearly indicated by bits of the old walls, and a few loose stones.

Though the Archdeacon felt no doubt as to the situation of Erghum's house archaeologists have shown some hesitation about it. But the deep digging of the field in preparation for ploughing (the first within living memory) that took place in the autumn of 1949, though it had no archaeological object in view, must surely have put an end to all doubts. For when men got to work the plough began to grate on big stones and they were forced to take to their spades. Soon they found not only a mass of stones, including a number of large sarsens, but also the clear outlines of a considerable building—or possibly of several buildings—with a paved path encircling the whole. Besides this main path there were three other paved paths each about two feet wide. The first path led to the south-east corner of the churchyard where the ditch is spanned by a bridge. The second took a straight line to Court Farm. The third, keeping to the west side of the field, looked as though it had once joined the footpath, disused now, that served as a short cut to Coate. Incidentally, the southern end of this path was, I think, the 'Church Way' described in the Court Book of 1682 as leading 'from the south part of Parsonage Croft to the north part of Pipers'.

The foreman, once a shepherd on Cannings Down, described the lay-out to me[4] and told how he had picked up a triangular stone ornament, about four inches long, such as might have crowned the top of a gateway. The main foundations remain sunk deep below the grass, and await a future ploughing to lay them bare once more.

THE MANOR HOUSE OF CANNINGS CANNONICORUM

On the west side of Chandlers' Lane, opposite a gate into the vicarage field, stands a handsome half-timbered farmhouse, now called the Old Manor, but formerly known as Parsonage Farm-house.[5]

Though it has been much restored and many additions made its roof timbers show that it almost certainly existed in the early seventeenth century. Moreover an Indenture, dated March 24, 1741[6] provides ample proof that it was formerly the Manor house of Cannings Cannonicorum. The Indenture makes John Weston, sub-tenant, responsible for a yearly rent of £200 to William Nicholas, lessee of the Dean and Chapter, and a descendant of Sir Oliver, Secretary of State to Charles I and Charles II, who had himself held the Manor in 1660.[7] John Weston was further required to deliver yearly, on the Feast of St Thomas (just in time for William's Christmas dinner, in fact) 'a good, swete, well-ordered chine of bacon, and a well-fed, young fat Hogg, one good, swete well-fed Turkey, and two good swete well-fed young Fowles of a reasonable size to the good liking of the said Nicholas'.

In addition Weston must provide 'meat, drink, lodging and horse meat for the officers of the Lord of the Manor (not exceeding 4 persons) to survey and keep courts there not more than twice in the year, and their stay not to exceed 2 nights and 2 days each time'.

This Indenture is probably more or less a replica of one that existed in the late sixteenth and early seventeenth century when other Westons also farmed the Manor.[8] So we may picture first William Weston (when George Ferebe arrived in Cannings) and then Thomas Weston, supplying the same chine of bacon, the same young fat hog and good sweet poultry on Christmas Eve to the Dean and Chapter's lessee, and also providing ample meals for the officers of the Manor when they came to hold their courts at Parsonage Farmhouse. Only these earlier Westons paid a considerably lower rent than their successors.

BOURTON MANOR AND THE ERNLES

By far the most important house in the village when George Ferebe came to Cannings was Bourton Manor, home of John Ernle, son and heir of Michael Ernle and of his wife, Mary Finnemore.

At first sight it will strike you as a most undistinguished-looking house, for in the last 100 years it has been so messed and mauled about that little of the original building is visible from the outside. During the latter part of the nineteenth century the roof of Cotswold slats, judged too heavy for the old beams, was replaced by slates and much of the ancient house was pulled down and a modern red-brick wing built. Only on the north and west remain a portion of the original stone walls, four feet thick at least.

Certainly nobody taking a quick glance would guess that here once lived a branch of a distinguished Wiltshire family. But if you stand outside the porch you will notice in the top portion of the triple-leaded window in the old greystone wall on your right two small diamond panes. One is engraved with a coloured coat-of-arms that includes a broad cross and an upturned sword; the other has the name 'Robert Ernly' written, probably with a diamond ring, in small beautiful lettering (perhaps Robert put in the 'y' so that he might finish off with a fine flourish!), followed by the words 'de victa fortuna fatu'.

That may serve to waken your interest in the Ernles. But before any more is said about them it is worth while to take a look inside their home. Here is much fine panelling both in the hall and on the staircase door. You see it again in the living-room, where the cupboards beside the fireplace reveal the depth of the outside walls. The dining-room is panelled throughout, and so are two of the bedrooms, where the doors are fitted with hinges of excellent craftsmanship. In John Ernle's day the whole house must have been of one piece. But in the mid-nineteenth century old Squire Ruddle—or the young Squire as he was then—thought there was too much of this dark wood about, stripped it from the walls and stacked it in one of his great thatched barns. Then, on a Sunday morning in Queen Victoria's Jubilee year, while he was at church, some children began playing with matches. The old barns went up in a terrific blaze, and the precious panelling added fuel to the flames. The Squire was called out of church but it was too late to do anything. Little remained of the barns but a smouldering heap of ashes.

Of the tradition that once there was a small monastery or monastic cell where Bourton Manor now stands I have already spoken. In his survey of his parish in 1860 Archdeacon Macdonald remarks that the orchards, walks and fishponds at Bourton Manor, 'sufficiently indicate the wealth and importance of the Ernle family'. Changes have taken place since then, and the walks are less evident, but the boundary banks still show it to have been a considerable property.

THE ERNLES

So much for the Manor. What of the family themselves? Four John Ernles[9] were squires at Bourton. The first one was a son of John of West Wittering in Sussex, who started the Wiltshire connection by his marriage with Joan, daughter of Simon Best,[10] heiress (through her Malwyn mother) to the manor of Etchilhampton. This first Wiltshire John was living at Bourton in 1539, when the Dean and Chapter leased to him 'the tithes of corn from the field called Burton and Eastonfield and also the tithes of lambs and wool'.[11]

It was his grandson, the third John, designated as 'our beloved son in Christ', to whom the churchwardens made over the 'Lady Bower'. He went into the White Horse Vale for his bride, Mary, daughter of William Hyde, squire of Denchworth, on the banks of the Childrey Brook between West Hanney and Goosey. Mary was one of the nineteen children,[12] eleven sons and eight daughters, who kneel behind their parents on two exquisite little brasses on the north wall of Denchworth Church. Part of her fifteenth century home still stands, and when she moved to Bourton it was to just such another small but substantial manor, standing in spacious grounds and possessing its own fish-ponds. Only instead of Wantage as her market town she shopped in Devizes. This third John, as his memorial in the Ernle Chapel tells us, 'departed this mortal life the first day Februarie in the year of our Lord God a thousand five hundred three score and eleven', and was succeeded by his son Michael, the Ernle who brought George Ferebe to Cannings.

Michael did well for himself and married two heiresses. The first was Mary, daughter of Roger Finnemore of Whetham.[13] To court her he had only to take a straight ride of about five miles across Roundway and down through Heddington and Heddington Wick. Michael was a person of consequence, both in his own right and through his marriage, and in 1579 he became Sheriff of Wiltshire. He and his wife evidently made their home for a time at Whetham while Roger Finnemore was still alive, since their eldest son was christened at Calne on May Day 1561. But they moved to Bourton after his father's death in 1571.

Mary died when she had borne Michael at least two sons and two daughters,[14] and not long afterwards he married his second heiress, Susan Hungerford, member of an important and widespread Wiltshire family, co-heir (with two sisters) of her father, Sir Walter, of Farleigh Castle on the Somerset-Wiltshire border, standing grand and high above the Frome. Her grandfather, another Sir Walter, was a real bad lot. He ill-used two wives and shut up his third in a tower for four years 'without comfort of any creature and under custody of my Lord's chaplain, Sir John à Lee, as hath once or twice poyson'd me. . . . He hath promised my Lord that he will soon rid him of me.'[15]

But in the end, as in all good stories, the villain is defeated and his victim avenged. This wicked Sir Walter was beheaded on Tower Hill in 1540 on a charge of treason, and his wife, free to marry again, knew happiness at last.

Susan Hungerford must have been quite young when she married Michael in 1577 because she lived on till 1646, out-lasting her husband by more than half a century. Michael, in his will (dated Nov. 1593), asked to be buried at Bishops Cannings, and bequeathed £2 for church repairs and £10 for the poor of the parish, to be paid to them after the funeral. But it does not appear that this ever took place in Cannings, so probably he died at Farleigh Castle. No doubt his son saw that both the church and the poor received their legacy. In all likelihood Michael's children by Susan were born at Bourton before the registers start. To her he left the corn growing in his fields and in 'his parsonage of tithes in Bourton and Easton'; half his plate and linen; half his Wiltshire estates, and as much timber as she needed from land at Poulshot. She should also have the right to occupy 'certain fields called Rowcroft, Newmeade, and Syndersmeade at a rent of 13s. 4d., and a little ground called Eston's Crofte'.[16]

If she married again—as indeed she did, twice over—'she shall keep her own jewels and apparel', and John Ernle, her stepson, is to pay her 200 marks yearly. In less than two years after Michael's death the registers record her marriage to John Marvin, and nine years later to Sir Carey Reynolds (probably of the Trowbridge family of that name).

Clearly Susan felt a deep affection for her Bourton home. In 1634 she appears in Tidcombe's survey of Cannings as 'the Lady Susan Reynolds who holds the Manor of Bourton'.[17] And here as a widow for a third time she stayed till her death in 1646, when Thomas Ferebe buried her in Cannings churchyard. Before she died, a very old lady, eighty-five at least, she saw troubled times in her quiet corner. Her shepherds on Roughridge Hill must often have brought their mistress tales of wild skirmishes. But at all events her sheep were not carried off to feed the King's army, as were those of Sir Edward Baynton from a piece of down nearby.

Of her children by Michael Ernle the eldest son, Walter, was buried in 1618 at Bath, only a few miles from Farleigh Castle.[18] His father left him his Sheriff's gold chain of office, but he died before he could ever hope to wear it. Edward, the second son, is buried in the Ernle Chapel. You will find an inscription to him, and another to his grandson, if you peer behind the old altar table. He settled at Etchilhampton Manor, inherited through his ancestress Agnes Malwyn.[19] It was a pleasant place to live in; quiet, but with the busy town of Devizes close at hand and his mother settled just over the hill. The old house stood where the Manor Farm stands today, near the wide water meadows. In two of them —'Threshletts' and 'Puddingmead'[20]—till the first quarter of the present century, grew hosts of fritillaries ('Turkey' or 'Ginnie-hen' Floures in Ferebe's day). They had flowered there as long as the oldest inhabitant in the late nineteenth century could remember and probably for many generations previously. If greedy people from Devizes had not dug up their roots to sell in the market they would be flowering still. On a May day their dark heads swaying among a glitter of marsh marigolds made an enchanting picture.

Edward Ernle's estate evidently dwindled, for when trouble with the Parliamentarians overtook him he petitioned against a fine of £400 on land that he declared was worth only £100 a year.[21] Moreover, he declared, he had done many a good turn for the Parliament party and had only acted for the King under compulsion. Whether his protest was heeded we don't know, but at all events he and his heirs continued at Etchilhampton well on into the eighteenth century. He himself did not live to see the return of the Royalists. In 1656 he died and was carried over the hill to 'the burying place of his fathers' in the Ernle Chapel.[22] But his son, Walter, was made a baronet in return for his father's services to the King. Both Walter and his son, another Walter, were buried at Cannings—in linen clothes instead of the prescribed woollen.

It is time to return to the John Ernle with whom we started, Ferebe's John, eldest son of Michael and Mary Finnemore. He was a man of thirty-two when Ferebe arrived in Cannings, and had married Margaret Haydock of 'Berie Towne'. Her family lived in the old greystone manor that stands so remotely among the low-lying fields north-east of the village of Broad Blunsdon—fields that during the Civil War were pounded by flying horsemen, as a trail of stirrups and spurs, still stored in an out-house, bear witness.

The Haydock coat-of-arms, depicting three fishes, looks as though originally their name was Haddock.

John and Margaret went to live at Bourton when Michael took up residence at Whetham. John evidently stayed on there after his father's death in 1594. A daughter (Mary) was buried at Cannings in 1595. After this Whetham claims him for part of the time. His twin sons, John and Michael,[23] were baptized at Calne in 1596. But the little Manor under the downs drew him back again. It is Ferebe who christens his next two sons, Edward and Charles (in 1599 and 1600), and he also buries young Robert in 1607. This Robert, I think, was John Ernle's first-born, and for a time his heir. That is why he was allowed the privilege of engraving his name and the Ernle crest on the window pane. He, too, like Mary, was almost certainly born at Bourton before the Cannings registers start at the end of 1591. So he was probably seventeen or eighteen when he died. It is pleasant to picture him and the other young Ernles playing in the great barns, taking rod and line to Fishwater, noting each spring the blossoming of the green hellebore beside the stream, watching the mill at work, or climbing Easton Hill in search of 'Bee Flowers'. And probably at Cannings they had their first lessons from the village schoolmaster, Hugh Gibbs, in the company of young Nicholases from Coate, Unwins from Horton, and sundry Ruddles and Slopers.

Perhaps George Ferebe took a share in Robert's education, taught him Latin and how to write that small clear hand. Ferebe, as the registers show, was himself a most skilful penman. It may be that sometimes the Ernle children stayed behind when their parents went to their larger house across the downs. Mary Ernle gave birth to more babies there, and altogether had twelve children.[24] Inevitably residence at Bourton became less and less frequent, and the life of Sir John and his family more centred at Whetham. His eldest son, John, married Philadelphia Hopton from Somerset and became father to the Sir John who was Chancellor of the Exchequer to James II and a friend of Aubrey's. This Sir John's first wife was Susan Howe from Down Ampney, near Cirencester. She kneels, a little girl in white marble touched with gold, with her parents and her seven brothers and sisters in the fascinating solitary little church in the water meadows.[25] His second wife was the widow of another close friend of Aubrey's, Charles Seymour of Marlborough.

This sixth John Ernle has a special interest for us because I believe it was he who handed on to Aubrey the story of Queen Anne's entertainment at Shepherds' Shore, told him no doubt by his father or his grandfather, George Ferebe's squire, who died in 1648 at the ripe age of 87. Sir John's own father went one better and lived to be 88.

The Bourton Ernles were indeed a long-lived and prolific race, and they married heirs or heiresses all over Wiltshire.[26] A Miss Ernle, celebrated for her beauty, who lived and died at Brimslade House in Savernake Forest in the eighteenth century,[27] was a great-granddaughter of Edward of Etchilhampton.

Lord Ernle, who, as Roland Prothero, wrote in so scholarly and attractive a fashion of English farming, was also a descendant of the country squires who kept their sheep on Easton Down and ran their small mill beside the baby Avon.

OTHER PEOPLE

Good Chandler

If it was too wild or wet for a walk on the downs or through the water meadows, then, of all the roads leading out of the village we loved best to go southwards along Chandler's Lane. On the right side just beyond the small thatched post-office, baby frogs swarmed about a little pond in early summer. On the right hand side grew a rose that flamed like a sunset among paler flowers. In a grass-grown lane on the left a glimpse could be caught at certain seasons of gipsies brooding darkly over their fire, filling a child's mind with a pleasurable mixture of excitement and fear. Further on, at the end of the lane in a very long field, grew the earliest primroses and the greatest profusion of white violets. Altogether there could be no doubt that the Lane had been planned by an unusually kind and pleasant person. It had been called 'Chandlers' for generations; that was all we knew about its name. So it was with surprise and delight that long afterwards I discovered 'Good Chandler' in the register. Thomas Ferebe buried him in 1638.

That he and his two brothers, Walter and Matthew, were responsible for the christening of the lane, is, of course, only guess-work. But it does seem pretty certain, since no other Chandlers are recorded (except a son for Walter) till nearly 100 years after Good's death. And the name was going strong in the seventeenth century, as the Court Books show. Mention of 'Chandlers's House' occurs in 1647, and of 'Chandler's Furlong' a little later. Un-doubtedly 'Chandler's Furlong' was the primrose field, because in the Dean and Chapter Survey of 1800, Upper, Middle and Lower Chandlers are all mentioned, and no other field was of a size to be so divided. Of 'Chandler's House' there is no word, so it dis-appeared before the survey was made. But once, in all likelihood, Good Chandler lived there, and no doubt kept watch on the foot-path that led to it. Some time after his death certain members of the Hommage were ordered to examine whether 'it be the King's way, or not'. The path, which exists no longer, would provide a short cut from the lane to the Devizes road.

Since the registers contain no reference to wife or children, it is likely that either Good was a bachelor or an old widower. Ever since I found his name he has been linked in my mind with the Lane.

NOTES TO CHAPTER VI

[1] *Q.S.G.R.*, ed. B. H. Cunnington.

[2] See Wilts Cuttings. XIV. 155. Source not given.

[3] Cal. Pat. (1377-81). Bishop Erghum was consecrated Bishop at Bruges. (*Faste Ecclesiae Anglicanae*. John Le Neve).

[4] His account is confirmed by J. Coombes and B. Dix (schoolmaster in Bishops Cannings at the time).

[5] So called in the Tithe Award map of 1841. The house is now occupied by Mr J. Coombes, whose family has farmed the Manor Farm since 1881.

[6] From Wilts News Cuttings, Vol. XVI, 211. Devizes Museum.

[7] *V.C.H.*, Vol. VII, 189.

[8] Court Baron for the Manor of Cannings Canonicorum, 16th June, 37 Elizabeth (1593) and also for November 24, 1595, and October 2, 1596, and April 18, 1620. In the County Archives at Trowbridge. See also Ch. IV.

[9] Ernle Family Tree at Whetham.

[10] Among the Whetham papers is one recording a grant in 1380 from a Simon Beste of all his lands in 'Cannynges Episcopi' to John Botelor 'Rector of Devizes', Thomas Newman, 'Chaplain of Devizes', and John Wakelynge, 'Chaplain of Canynges'. This shows that the Cannings connection (by marriage) goes back very early.

[11] Whetham Papers. He married Anne Darell of Collingbourne Kingston.

There is a brass to her mother, Joanna, but one to her father, Constantine, has vanished. The daughter of John and Anne married into the Goddard family when she became the second wife of Thomas of Ogbourne and Upham. Will proved in 1538. (This Thomas must not be confused with a later Thomas who married a Giffard and died in 1597.) A striking monument in Aldbourne Church shows Thomas a burly figure in armour, and Anne, small and meek in a black dress. Beside them kneel five sons and two daughters. I am indebted to Miss R. Goddard for information about Thomas of Ogbourne. The oldest son of John Ernle and Anne Darrell married Lucy Cook, daughter of a Salisbury merchant.

[12] But six children must have died in infancy since their names are not in 'The Visitation of Berks' (1566). *The Geneologist*, I, 14.

[13] The name is still attached to a bridge between his house and Cuff's Corner, to an aisle in Calne church, and to a town charity.

[14] Visitation of Wilts., 1623.

[15] In her petition (addressed to a Minister of State and quoted in Burke's History of English Commoners) she says that owing to her fear of tasting any food or drink brought her by this chaplain she would have starved but for the charity of certain poor women who 'brought to my great window in the night such meat or drink as they had and gave me for the love of God'.

[16] Copy of the Will of Sir Michael Ernle in the library of W.A.M. at Devizes.

[17] Presumably from Henry Blackborrow who bought it from John Ernle in 1630. (*V.C.H.*, VII., 189.)

[18] His epitaph runs:

An Ernle Hungerford heer lieth in grave
More THEN THINE owne (O earth) THOU maist not have.
His earthie part his body, That is thine,
His heavenlie, his sowle that is part divine
Is heavens right, there doth it live and raigne
In joy and bliss for ever to remaine.
His body in his bosome earth must keepe
Till such as rest in hope shall rise from sleepe
Then body joind with sowle for ever shall—'

(The last line is completely covered.)

[19] In Etchilhampton Church a striking tomb may safely be ascribed to the Malwyns. It dates from about 1460, and on it are the recumbent figures of a knight and of his lady in square head-dress and long cloak. Of the twelve children some raise their hands in prayer and some hold discs.

[20] The name 'Puddingmead' derives from an ancient custom, whereby the farmer's wife sent along a huge pudding when the men had mown the meadow as far as a certain tree. Then down they sat in the shade to eat it. (Information from H. Crees, whose grandfather farmed at Etchilhampton.)

[21] 'As to his personal estate,' he said he had '8 cows, 6 oxen, 5 young beasts and about 4 score sheep.' (Fosse's *Judges of England*, see *W.A.M.* XI.)

[22] Bishops Cannings Registers. Etchilhampton also records his burial. After these only two more Ernles were brought to the former 'Lady Bower' —Edward's younger son, Michael (of Brimslade), who married one of the Withers, and Martha, a daughter born to the first Sir Walter and his wife twenty-four years after their eldest child.

[23] Of Michael, the younger twin, Aubrey writes: 'After he had spent

some time at the University of Oxford, he betook himself to a militarie life in the Low Countries where he became so proficient that, at his return into England at the beginning of the civil warres, King Charles I gave him the commission of a Colonel . . . and shortly afterwards he was made Governor of Shrewsbury. . . . His garrison at Shrewsbury being weakened by drawing out a great part of them before the batell at Marston Moore, the townsmen ploted and betrayed his garrison to the Parliament soldiers. He was slain there in the market-place about the time of the battle of Marston Moore.' (*Natural History of Wilts.*)

[24] Two sons, Fynamore and Thomas, went to Magdalen Hall. Thomas became Rector of Eversley.

[25] She is also commemorated in a black marble slab on the floor of St Leonard's Church at Broad Blunsdon, where she died in 1669. There, too, Philadelphia, her daughter, figures with her husband, Sir John Pottenger, Headmaster of Winchester, on a handsome tablet by Scheemaker.

[26] Among these was Jane, daughter of Michael and Susan, who married Sir Anthony Hungerford of Down Ampney.

[27] Vol. I of the oldest *W.A.M.*

CHAPTER VII

The Drews and
'Life's Farewell'

A T Rangebourne Manor,[1] Southbroom, then in Bishops Cannings parish, lived close friends of both George and Thomas Ferebe. These were the Drews,[2] a family who held land in Bishops Cannings from 1498 till round about 1689, also in Southbroom, and owned two mills (pulled down in the last century) east of the Potterne road. They gave their name to a much frequented pond near Devizes.[3]

John was head of the family in the early years of the seventeenth century, and between him and George Ferebe existed a strong friendship. 'Love and duty,' says George in his funeral sermon for John, 'brought me often to him.' He relates how, when his friend was sinking fast, a messenger arrived to beg him to come at once and 'comfort his heart'. In his eulogy of John Drew Ferebe gives a picture of a simple, dignified gentleman, who expressed himself 'in a plaine-meaning fashion, without curious and affected complements', and loved also to dress plainly. 'Humerous and fantasticall vanitie of changeable, and chargeable, suites of clothes; silken outsides on the backe, shewes of swelling insides at the heart, outward ensignes of inward pride—these were most distastefull (I may say hatefull) to him for ever.' John Drew was also a kindly landlord, 'not racking or gripping to grind the faces of the poore'.

Nor is it likely that he was hard on poachers since he himself connived at the practice at least once. His servant, John Bishop, confessed that at five o'clock on a May morning he had coursed a young stag near Rowde Marsh with a stray greyhound (which he conveniently chanced to meet!) and had driven it to 'Rowdes

Swillin Meade', where the dog killed it. Later he took it on horse-back to John Drew's house 'at the Vize Greene'.[4] A little poaching by their servants was a common practice among country gentle-men in those days and it is unlikely that the respected John Drew himself incurred any penalty.

'John was commendably courteous to strangers,' the sermon continues, 'very kind to honest passengers, truly comfortable to neighbours, dearly tender to his friends, exceeding merciful to his enemies, admirably patient in all his crosses.'

What these crosses were we are not told. Ferebe only enlarged on his blessings. 'Blessings embroydered, enfolded upon him. God from heaven poured down blessing upon blessing with a full home, temporal, corporal, spirituall; faire possessions, propagation of a sweete progenie, children, children's children.'

Of his fair possessions I have spoken already. As to his 'sweete progenie', though he is recorded as having but two children him-self, Robert his heir, who married the daughter of a wealthy London alderman, gave him grandchildren in full measure—six sons and five daughters. Robert was a prominent person in Devizes, an alderman, and its representative in Parliament three times.[5]

John was never so public a figure, and this funeral sermon tells us more about him than we learn anywhere else. As a Drew and father of a burgess, it was natural that though he lived in South-broom his funeral should take place at St John's, the most im-portant church in the town, Bishop Roger's Church,[6] standing massive and splendid above the western vale, creation of the same fine brain that built the Castle. George Ferebe, when he mounted the fifteenth century oak pulpit, would assuredly face a large congregation that included the Mayor and Aldermen. He had achieved a reputation as a preacher, and many apart from re-lations and friends of the dead man would flock to hear him. They must have felt amply rewarded both by the length and quality of the sermon that followed. It ran to over 9,000 words, certainly lasted for more than an hour, and was full of the ornate images, the classical and biblical allusions, the virtuosity, so dear to seventeenth century preachers. Though not by any means a John Donne, George Ferebe understood how to move and startle his listeners. His text he took from *Second Book of Samuel* Chapter

XIV : 'For we must needs die.' He recalls dramatically the story of incest and murder, so singularly inappropriate to quiet, God-fearing John Drew, from which the words derive. Absalom has bidden his brothers to a sheep-shearing feast to avenge the viola-tion of his sister Tamar by one of them. 'A bloody banket,' com-ments the preacher, '. . . a short, sharp meale, the dinner done as soon as begun. Every man . . . stands wondrously amazed, the Author and the actors flye.' Finally a wise woman, interceding with King David for Absalom, uses the words of the text. One by one Ferebe deals with each of them. 'For' provides the reason why John Drew's family and friends patiently accept his loss. Noah, Nebuchadnezzar, David, are all cited as examples—'the more the waters increased the higher the Arke was mounted. So these waters of trouble, the nearer they are the nearer they lift us up to heaven.' It is trouble alone that humbles the proudest Nebu-chadnezzar. David cries, 'It is good for me that I have been in trouble.' 'A vine,' comments Ferebe, 'the more it is pruned the faster it sprouteth. Pepper the more it is braised the hotter it tasteth. . . . Thus God's children have their woes and huge ones too. . . . Howsoever, they are good for mee and good for thee.' From an old Latin verse he translates, 'It is health for high mortals to be whipt with heaven's high rod.'

'Wee' illustrates the universality of death. In reply to David's 'question questionless'—'what man is he that shall not see death?' he marshals first Solomon, then Paul, then Alexander with his plumes and his triumphs, and Croesus with his heaped-up riches. He asks his listeners for patience while he likens human destiny to 'witty chess play, which it doth prettily resemble. There is the King, Queene, Bishop, and the rest ranked in their orders even to the lowest pawns, and while the game holds out the highest stands subject to the checke.' From his graphic description of the game it seems likely that Ferebe played it personally; perhaps with John Drew himself or with John Ernle at Bourton Manor.

When he reaches the words 'must needs' he grows eloquent on man's weakness. 'There is an old saying, "Neede maketh the old wife trot"; she will trot for life, I warrant you.' The certainty of death makes 'old and young trudge and trot for life, not for this life but for that life which endureth ever.' The world resembles 'a bitter unsavorie sea, which we must needs sail through in this

slender barke of our bodies'. It is 'a thorny, stonie plot, ill ground
for a race, yet we must needs run it out to the last poste, Deathe.
. . . This is the King's highway, no way but this common way to
the Court where the King is'. Reaching now this final word of his
text 'die', he, true child of the seventeenth century, grows still
more eloquent and dramatic. 'Most men never yield till they must.'
Every remedy is tried to save a sick man. 'Physicians and surgeons
must come with their purges and plasters; the cook in the kitchen
must make broathes and cullases; the hostess seeke her closet for
the sovereignest restoratives, servants trudge to and fro, clothes
must be heated, beddes warmed, heades held fast, bodies bolstered
up, standersby pitying, friends sighing, children mourning, their
eyes streaming, their hands wringing, their hearts aking. Lord,
what a stir is here and to how little purpose! . . . We must
needes die. . . . These our Corporal Copyholds are not our
inheritance.'

At this point, led on by Job's simile of man's life springing up
and dying like a flower, Ferebe cannot resist an allusion to Bath
(for this sermon was preached the year after Queen Anne's visit).
'Pardon me in the comparison,' he says, 'that wondrous place
giveth me a cause to love it well.' For a moment he forgets death
and John Drew, and sees himself once more at Shepherd's Shore
on a summer day meeting the Queen as she returns from 'that
wondrous place'. 'Job determineth the time, as the men of Bath
reckon the seasons. . . . There is no talke there of Midsummer
and as little of mid-winter. All is spring and fall there.'

But the next moment Death is back in the picture. 'Let life
have leave to flaunt it and brave it and pompe it awhile on the
stage of this world . . . but Death at the last . . . grimly comes
in with a terrible Epilogue.' John Drew, having received the sacra-
ment and 'expressed such detestation of his sinnes that nothing
more can be expected of a Christian', is waiting to be laid in his
grave.

Ferebe calls his sermon 'Life's Farewell' and in his introduction
to the printed copy,[7] he writes, 'This funeral sermon, preached
upon the death of a Gentleman, my parishioner and neighbour,
being by the importunity of some, brought to the Press (I hope)
for the benefit of all.'

It looks as if copies were fairly widely distributed, but as far as we know the only one in existence is that in The Bodleian. Certainly at least one copy went to Lord Knollys, to whom the sermon is dedicated. This was the man who, in George Ferebe's own words, had encouraged him both 'in his raw and riper studies', and who had taken a friendly interest both in himself and his brothers, both at Oxford and after they left.

The author ends his introduction in true seventeenth century style. 'If from your Lordship it obtain the least approbation, I have my heart's desire, which shall ever spend itself in prayer to God for the completing here, and crowning hereafter of your Lordship's manifold graces and virtues.

> Your Lordship's most bounden and dutiful Chaplain,
> George Ferebe.'

NOTES TO CHAPTER VII

[1] *W.A.M.*, XLII, 102. Rangebourne was burnt down in the Civil War.

[2] The first association of Drews and Ferebes took place when William Ferebe, a priest, attended a convention with Lawrence Drew in 1398. Rymer, VIII, 54. Quoted by Arch. Macdonald, *W.A.M.*, VI.

[3] See Appendix for more about Drew's Pond.

[4] *Q.S.G.R.*, p. 28.

[5] The elegant silver loving-cup at the Town Hall bears his name.

[6] Though this is now disputed, and the church assigned to a period after Bishop Rogers' death, we may still believe that the initial inspiration was his.

[7] *Life's Farewell*. Printed by Edwin Griffin for Ralph Mabbe, 1615. Copy in the Bodleian, Oxford.

CHAPTER VIII

Village Life

EDUCATION AND HEALTH

Education

F E W of Ferebe's flock could read or write. Even some members of such important yeoman families as the Ruddles or the Nashes only signed their names with a mark.

Yet there had existed in Bishops Cannings a school at least as early as the beginning of the fifteenth century.[1] We have seen how two young Unwins left it to become scholars of Winchester, one in the early fifteenth, and one in the early sixteenth century. Hugh Gibbs, father of two Susanahs, was the schoolmaster when Ferebe arrived. No mention of him occurs after the birth of a third daughter and in 1631 his place is taken by 'Mr Henry Hamand'.

In the later troubled years of Thomas Ferebe's time it may well be that the school came to an end. At all events no further entry of 'schoolmaster' occurs. But in its more flourishing days the young Ernles, and Snells, the Cooks and Westons, and, presumably, George Ferebe's own two Thomases and his brother's sons likewise received their education there—unless their fathers chose to teach them at home.

What kind of school it was we can only guess, but probably it began as a little chantrey school in connection with the Lady Bower chapel.

Health

That the people of Cannings were a healthy lot on the whole, worked hard all their lives and lived in many cases to a ripe old age, was due to their own splendid constitutions and good home-grown, though restricted, food. Yet even so the expectation of life for the period was very short compared with ours. In spite of such people as 'Old Henry Baily' and 'Thomas Sloper'—the nonagenarian—the expectation of life was only about thirty years because of excessive infant mortality. The wonder is that so many babies survived, considering their tight swaddling clothes and the suffocating atmosphere in which they were reared. No windows opened in cottages, and there was little personal washing. Drinking water, too, was often contaminated by polluted streams and ditches, uncleansed by those responsible. In Cannings people were hauled up from time to time for making 'a mucksome (or dung-heap) . . . to ye greate anoyence of the Kinge leige people', like John Payne in Devizes—whose offence was the greater in that he made it in the Market Place.[2]

For treatment in time of sickness country people relied largely on herbal or other homely remedies, many of them extremely unpleasant. For example, for those suffering from measles in the sheep-rearing district of Wilts., it was recommended that a sheep be laid on the bed 'because these creatures are easily infected and draw the venom to themselves'. In the mid-nineteenth century there were still some who followed the repulsive custom of swallowing live sheep ticks for rheumatism. As for the herbs in common use, at a glance at any old herbal book of the period proves that they were legion. Yarrow, comfrey, nettles, elder, from the hedges and ditches, wormwood and mugwort from the farmyards, eyebright from the downs, valerian from the bogs round Laywoods, coltsfoot from upland fields for coughs (still gathered by Cannings women in the late nineteenth century)—these and dozens of others would be in continual use. Probably there was always some old woman in the village extra wise about herbs, or a pedlar might boost a remedy in his 'fardle', or be ready to pull out teeth when required. Sometimes a local bone-setter was visited, as in the case of an unhappy girl who appeared before the Devizes magistrates in 1615. Her parents had taken her for treatment of 'a greefe in her necke'. When she shrank away from the bone-setter and 'did hold her necke on thone side', he 'with bothe his hands did turne her necke upright, and in doing thereof he harde some of the veines or sinews of her necke goe racke'. Yet it was the girl who was punished![3]

In Devizes, Marmaduke Burd, nephew by marriage to Griffin

Nicholas, practised in Thomas Ferebe's time and probably in George's later days. Cannings folk no doubt called at his surgery on Market days, and the well-to-do received personal visits from him.

Plague. A bad outbreak of plague in Cannings neighbourhood in the autumn and winter of 1603-1604 was declared to have been spread from London by 'the wonderinge upp and downe the country of idle and loyteringe vagabonds and other loose persons'.

Early in 1604 George Ferebe, like all his fellow parsons, must read aloud in church an Order from the Justices, which, after complaining that 'The Constables, Tithingmen, and Hedboroughes with in this County have been very remisse in thexecucon of the statute' (i.e. for the punishment of such idlers and vagabonds) enjoined that in future they, as well as 'other officers and ministers' should use their best endeavours to bring to justice these infection-spreading persons.[4] Even those with the plague on them were to be whipped every day.

Another virulent outbreak swept Devizes and its neighbourhood in 1607, resulting in many deaths. John Noyes, M.P. for Calne at one time, wrote from London begging his wife to go 'any whither than tarry at Calne',[5] and at Chippenham the market was closed and no fairs allowed.

Anyone who showed the slightest pity for a nameless wanderer was looked on as a public enemy, like the husbandman a few miles east of Cannings who sheltered a woman and her child for three nights in 1605. As John Taylor, the 'waterman' poet, put it in the preface to *The Fearful Summer* (which refers to an outbreak in 1625): 'This was the time when a man with a night-cap at noon would have frighted a whole parish out of its wits.'

Probably the people of Bishops Cannings went into the town as little as possible at such times, and the market place would present a far less lively picture than usual. Though Ferebe's duties took him to St James he would encourage his wife to stay at home. Local weavers suffered much from the pervading fear. The clothiers refused to accept their work, so that 'no means were left unto them . . . to get their lyvinge unless it shall please God very shortly to stay the infection thereof', and arrangements for their relief were made by the Justices.

Perhaps because they shunned contact with the town Cannings folk do not appear to have suffered high mortality during this early outbreak. But during the later one of 1636-37, as has been seen, there was a noticeable increase in the death roll.

SOCIAL OCCASIONS

Going to Market

Though but a small town in those days Devizes had long held (and has continued to hold) an important market. 'The market is very celebrate,' says Leland when he journeyed through Wiltshire about 1540. 'On Thursdays a very plentifull market of everything'. The best for fish' (from Poole) in the county,' says John Aubrey some hundred years later. To this market the people of Bishops Cannings have flocked for hundreds of years, and in George Ferebe's day Thursday mornings would see a little crowd journeying on horse or donkey-back, in small rough carts, but mostly on foot, along the upper road by West End, or down Chandler's Lane, or following the lost footpath across Spratts and through the cornfields. Once on the highroad their way led past St James's Church, a smaller building then with a tower not more than a hundred years old, and past the Crammer, probably a corruption of 'Cranmere' (=Cranes' Pool) and thus linked for them with their own 'Stork's Meads'.[6] Close by on the spacious Green they gathered from time to time for the Fair—the Fair granted by King John to the lepers in Spital Street 'on the eve of the feast of the Blessed Dionysius' (St Denis), and one that was a perquisite of their own Lord of the Manor, the Bishop of Salisbury; as well as the Midsummer fair held 'on the vigil, the day, and the morrow of St John the Baptist for ever'.

Journeying on through the Brittox or along Monday Market Street they came in to the wide but far emptier Market Place. Here no exuberant goddess crowned the Corn Exchange, no sober Victorian gentleman stood above a fountain guarded by eagles and lions, no neo-Gothic monument proclaimed the dramatic death of a blasphemous woman. But in 1615 they had the excitement of seeing the new 'measuring-house near the corn market' growing up, and 'the new market-house for wool and yarn and for the holding of the Sessions of the County'.[7]

Devizes possessed a flourishing wool market supplied by local weavers, including a few from Cannings. So not only did Cannings folk buy their fish and other food-stuffs here but also such cloth as they did not weave for themselves at home.

Apart from watching the growth of these new buildings there was the more doubtful pleasure of seeing men and women whipped round the town 'till their backes doe bleed'—a man who stole a pair of shoes from a cordwainer, a woman who carried off an old cauldron, and other such petty thefts. They could also watch the ducking of unfortunate misdoers, tied to the cucking-stool, in the Crammer. The ponds in Cannings were barely large enough for that.

Finally, before the market-goers went home some of them refreshed themselves with the methgelin, or spiced mead, for which Aubrey tells us Devizes was noted. I wonder if they could also buy the equally famous cheese-cakes and, in mid-Lent, the Simnel cakes? But those may belong to a later period.

Tan Hill Fair

'On St Anne's Hill, vulgarly called Tan Hill,'[8] wrote Aubrey, 'every Year is kept a great fair within an old camp.' 'The commodities,' he goes on, 'are sheep, oxen, and fineries. This faire would be more considerable, but that Bristowe Faire happens at the same time.'

But even so, Tan Hill Fair was famous for miles around, and for at least 500 years, and probably a good deal longer, it was a great event in the lives of the country people.

By a Charter dated Nov. 5, 1499, the Abbess of St Mary's, Winchester, was granted a yearly fair in the Parish of All Cannings 'in a place called Charlborough Down by Wansdyke on the feast and morrow of St Anne'.[9] By the old reckoning that was July 26, or August 6 by the new (or, after the Reformation, on the previous Saturday if St Anne's Day fell on a Sunday). Only once in all its long life is there any record of its omission, and this was in 1637 when, because of the bad outbreak of plague in Devizes and the neighbourhood the town burgesses decided to ban it. Captain Nicholas of All Cannings was compensated for the loss of his dues by the payment of £2 10s. to him by order of the Mayor.[10]

The people of Bishops Cannings flocked to the Fair in the last part of the nineteenth century, and they surely did the same when George and Thomas Ferebe were alive. Some went for business and some for fun. It was a great social occasion. Gentlemen, yeomen and smallholders, with their wives and children—Richard Snell and John Ernle, Thomas Withers and Thomas Slop; the Pottles, the Bellys, the Dickes, and many another Cannings family—all would be there. Farmer Ruddles were riding up from Easton or across Horton Down in the sixteenth and seventeenth centuries, and were still doing it when George Ferebe had been dead nearly three hundred years. Slowly the great padded knickerbockers of Ferebe's farmers gave place to the close-fitting breeches of the late nineteenth century, their doublets to three-quarter riding coats, and their wide-brimmed hats to hard high-crowned bowlers or green billycocks. No doubt they were served with the same hearty meal of cold meats and cheese eaten inside a wooden hut on the hill-top as in the nineteenth century. Ferebe's John Shepherd went up in clothes spun from the wool of the sheep he tended; his successors in stout smocks,[11] and *their* successors in the great blue cloaks of which I have spoken. And along with the crowd which hurried up Easton Hill as the sun rose (for the Fair always started very early), it is safe to assume went George Ferebe and his family.

As they gained the top of the ridge they would see, as did people of a later day, flocks of sheep making for Tan Hill from north, east and west, across the sea of downs, or climbing up from Pewsey Vale. The same clouds of white dust would rise from thousands of small hooves, the same musical clamour of sheep-bells and shouts of shepherds fill the air. Many of these latter had been on the move since the first streak of daylight. They came from perhaps twenty, thirty, or forty miles away and rested through the night with their flocks at some downland farm; or lay in a sheltered hollow or the lee of a clump of trees.

As for the sheep themselves they were the old horned Wiltshire sheep till Southdowns and Hampshire Downs superseded them. Nor was it only sheep that gathered from all points of the compass on Tan Hill. People knew how to walk in those days, and the Fair drew them from near and far. Up from the south and east came the inhabitants of Pewsey, Huish, Wilcot, Woodborough, the Altons, Stanton St Bernard, All Cannings, and from other little villages in the Vale. Parties from the Kennet Valley, from Avebury, Yatesbury, Cherhill, Calstone and Calne climbed from the north. Across Roundway Down and along Wan's dyke trooped others who would have included such solid people as the Drews and the Nicholases.

In the latter part of the nineteenth century an old Devizes woman walked over the hills carrying a bucketful of cooked broad beans. Arrived at the Fair, she sat herself down on the grass, waved a large two-pronged fork and cried aloud, 'A penny a stab! Come my dears, and try your luck! There's a fine prize for him who stabs the most.' The man who talked of her remembers as a hungry little boy how good the beans tasted. No doubt her counterpart existed in the seventeenth century.

But in those earlier days there was one section of the community who, if present at all, would have been represented in but small numbers. I refer to gipsies. 'Egyptians,' we know, were harshly dealt with in the sixteenth and early seventeenth centuries and continually chivvied by the village constables. In the nineteenth century, however, they played a characteristic and important part at the Fair. Dark ragged children peered out above the furze bushes; old women sat on the steps of their caravans; younger women offered gingerbread, clothes pegs, haberdashery. The men rode round displaying their horses and bargaining cunningly. Old Doctor Maurice from Marlborough and many another connoisseur of a good horse regularly bought from them. Excellent cheeses, too, were sold at the Fair, and barrels of beer and cider brought up in trucks. The inspiriting company, the sun and wind, the long early morning walk, combined to make people thirsty, and it is safe to guess that in Ferebe's day as in later years there would be certain countrymen who returned home in a strangely roundabout way.

Now no Fair brings Tan Hill to life, for it finally died after slow decay in 1925.[12] No sheep feed on the summit, though a flock is usually to be found on the northern slopes where they are safe from the shells that on certain days scream overhead. But at other times, when the hill is left in peace, it is still a glorious place for a walk. Below you on the one hand stretches Pewsey Vale, where the Kennet and Avon canal makes a thread of brightness between dusky copses and innumerable elms. And beyond the chequered

fields and the trees, that grow ever bluer and mistier, rises the
Plain, firm and tangible when the west wind blows but trans-
formed by an east wind into a remote rainbow-coloured kingdom.
Northwards, Wansdyke climbs and falls and the Kennet villages
raise their heads from among more massed elms. Peewits call,
kestrels gather sometimes seven or eight at a time, and a buzzard
may soar overhead. At dusk the high sweet note of the stone
curlew is sometimes heard, but far less frequently than it used to
be. But what none of us will ever see or hear again are the great
musical flocks moving up to the summit or the gipsy caravans
with their strings of horses and ragged children; all the bustle
and stir, the laughter and the shouting of a great occasion; the
participation in an event that brought rollicking life to the old
hill for one day in every year.

NOTES TO CHAPTER VIII

[1] *W.A.M.*, VI, 131-32.

[2] *Q.S.G.R.*, ed. B. H. Cunnington, p. 53.

[3] ibid, p. 3.

[4] ibid, pp. 10, 11.

[5] Waylen, *History of Devizes*, p. 77.

[6] Alternatively it may have been so called after Dame Cramer, who once lived at Southbroon and gave land to Bishops Cannings.

[7] Devizes Chamberlain's Accounts.

[8] *Natural History of Wilts*. In the last part of his statement he is mistaken. The nearest camp, Rybury, lies three-quarters of a mile away and is not part of Tan Hill.

Though St Anne has been the accepted saint of the hill for a very long time it is probable that it took its name originally from a local land-owner. In a survey made in 903 of the parish of Stanton Berners (Stanton St Bernard) occurs 'Anne's Crundall' (an old word meaning a tumulus or barrow), and in a Stanton Charter there are 'Anne's Thorn, and 'Anne's Stone'. In mediaeval times this land-owning Anne may well have been promoted to sainthood. The corruption of her name is found again in two fields not far away—'Little Tan House Pasture' and 'Great Tan House Pasture'.

[9] Quoted by R. B. Pugh from *Cal. of Charter Rolls, 1427-1516*, p. 273.

[10] Devizes Chamberlain's Accounts.

[11] Late in the nineteenth century a smock was sometimes tested by Cannings men on its ability to hold a bowl of 'pap' (bread-and-milk) without the liquid oozing through it.

[12] In 1911 a 21-year lease of the tolls and profits were offered at a rack-rent by Ferris and Duckeridge but no one bid.

CHAPTER IX

Outside the Parish

CALSTONE

WHEN, in the year 1600, Lawrence Jones, vicar of the neighbouring parish of Calstone (or Knarstones) died, Sir Thomas Edward and his wife Anna, patrons of the living, presented it to George Ferebe[1]—a welcome gift. It added quite a bit to his income and involved a pleasant ride or walk of only three miles across the downs. When he stood on the Roman Road 800 feet up he would see only a shadowy glimpse of the tiny village buried among elms between two ramparts of downs. Then he would drop by the old 'Burning Path' through the great south field of Calstone Manor into his new parish. A map at Bowood shows it and the corresponding North field, rising towards Oldbury Castle, each cut into innumerable strips.[2] Traces of them are visible still.

I don't know which is the more attractive—Calstone seen hiding among the trees, or Calstone when you have left the downs, passed the little solitary church, and entered the village. Here is no street or concentration of houses, but just three farms and their attendant cottages scattered in delightfully fortuitous fashion above the Marden and its tributaries. Sixty years ago it looked almost the same and probably has not greatly changed since Ferebe's day. The astonishing pace at which the Marden grows is unmatched by any other Wiltshire stream. Gently, unobtrusively, it steals from a tangle of trees and undergrowth. Yet within a few yards, during a wet season, it is a lively brook with a voice once plainly heard as you approached from the northern downs. The voice must have grown fainter now because of the deep borings on Oldbury Castle and other places that are stealing the water away.

Till recent years a great sheep-washing took place annually near the source. On some warm morning in late May or early June thousands of Hampshire Downs flocked over the hills from miles away, including many of our Cannings sheep. For nowhere else in all the country round was such a supply of running water to be found, and there were hatchways to supply the necessary depth. These sheep-washings had been going on as long as the grandfathers of the oldest inhabitants in the late nineteenth century could remember, and pretty certainly existed in Ferebe's day. His interest in shepherds must have led him to them sometimes.

When the newly-born Marden has wound for about a quarter of a mile through deepening undergrowth, barricaded on the north by a steep wall of limestone, it spreads out into an enchanting pool—blue-green because of its bed of clay. Only at a certain time of year a magenta, fungus-like scum covers its surface. Owing to the speed and liveliness of the little river there were till recent times a succession of mills along its banks. First there was a paper mill, then a flour mill, then a mill where mops were made from long strands of sheeps' wool, followed by a second flour mill. After that came 'Splays' where balls of whitening for hearthstones and doorsteps were moulded from chalk off the downs. The chalk was put in water in a huge round trough fitted with metal arms and rotated by an ancient horse, and the resulting thick white mixture shaped into balls by women. But far more important in the eyes of children was the tea-garden at 'Splays'. After eating delicious home-made bread-and-butter beside the stream, which here widened into a shallow pool, they could float about in a large flat boat 'as safe as a church', according to an advertisement. But all that is a thing of the past.

Though 'Splays' and the mop and paper mills did not exist in the early seventeenth century, there was at least one flour mill, and probably more. Fullers also used the stream, for the village lay within the main wool-making district of Wilts. A Calstone fuller was indicted as 'a comen bareter' (baret A.S.=strife) 'a troubler . . . a comen disturber, a lybell maker against his neighbour to the great disturbance and unquyetness of the said neighbour', in 1606.[3] And in 1603 John Mather, a Calstone miller lodged a complaint against William Salt, who forced his way through his property 'against the King's Imperial Crown and dignity'.[4]

Calstone Church, dedicated like Ferebe's other church to the Virgin Mary, may seem insignificant in comparison, yet small as are the proportions, the unity of design, and the tall western arch, are remarkably pleasing. Moreover the situation at the foot of the down in a little hummocky meadow has great charm, and through the clear glass windows you may look up at the long green slope that leads to the Roman Road. Before the restoration in 1885 the seating in the church consisted of very ancient, worm-eaten oak pews, some of which were fitted with narrow ledges fixed to their outer ends. On these the small boys were planted well under the eye not only of the schoolmaster but of the entire congregation. An old inhabitant remembers seeing them sitting there.[5] So old and decayed were the pews when removed that we may justly believe that the people of Calstone sat in them, and also the boys on the same uncomfortable perches, when George Ferebe took the services. Though the small tower could scarcely hold more than its three bells there is an ancient grievance, remembered still by old people, that wicked Cannings folk came over the hill and stole away their peal. One cast by John Wallis and inscribed 'Give God the Glory', was hung in 1603, almost certainly through the zeal of George Ferebe. Long afterwards Calstone inhabitants seem to have persuaded themselves that the other Wallis bells hanging in Bishops Cannings tower had in fact been filched from them.

There was always some rivalry between the two villages and Calstone loved to taunt the big village across the downs with their ridiculous steeple. The big village, in its turn, thought Calstone as a place good only for the washing of sheep.

Among the papers at Bowood is a most interesting document that helps to reconstruct the life in Calstone while Ferebe was rector there. This is a copy of *The Customs of the Manor of Calstone* dated 1621.[6]

There were nineteen copyholders at this time. One of the customs gave the Lord the right, on the death of a copyholder whose 'heriot' is uncertain, to take his heir's best beast, or failing that 'his best gives'. The use of 'gives' here is misleading since the Lord, deprived of his beast, might seize forcibly the best piece of household stuff belonging to the tenant. Calstone, as has been seen, numbered many weavers, and a roll of homespun often formed part of their possessions. Another custom lays it down that the farmer shall provide the men working for him between May and Midsummer with 'the dyett and wages here following. . . . For the plow folkes bread, cheese and beere, to be brought them in the fields; and for the driver of the plow toopence a day . . . and the farmer is to allow and provid the labourers sufficient hott meat for their breakfasts and dinners, and sufficient bread and beere at every throughs', i.e. at the end of the day when they were 'through' with their work.[7] The spelling in this old document is unusually homely—the work of men shut away in their village under the downs who seldom read anything and wrote as little as possible. In Wiltshire language they were 'poor spellards'.

In Ferebe's day the Lord of the Manor was Lionel Duckett, M.P. for Calne, who, though his principal home was at Pinhills close to the town, sometimes occupied his Manor house at Calstone,[8] built above the Marden on the spot where now stands the Manor Farm. Though he died unmarried, it seems likely that he fathered a number of boys in Calstone, all of whom were called after him and to whom he bequeathed forty shillings each when they came of age. The Ducketts were the big people. But there was a humbler, and possibly more useful Calstone family, who have persisted there for many generations. These were the Greens, famous throughout the countryside as makers of dew-ponds. The daughter of one of the last of these remembers how her father always talked as though there had never been a time when Greens were not carrying on their trade. The dew-pond where the Moonrakers diddled the Excise Officers would have been their work. Sometimes they came driving home at night in a small horse-cart. Sometimes they slept in barns, where rats gnawed their shoes, and continued their work at daybreak. Even in Ferebe's day it is possible that as he walked the downs he saw a little gang of Greens busy laying the foundations of rubble, straw and slaked lime. Their ponds may be traced on many a lonely hilltop and one above Calstone still holds a little water.

George Ferebe remained rector of the village for twenty-three years, and during his visits he would see other parishioners working their mills, plying their looms, labouring on their strips in the wide upland fields.

As they walked doggedly through the sticky chalk on wet days, with the wind sweeping down the valley or off the downs, the name 'Long Sorrow', given to one of the steepest northern fields, must have seemed strangely apt.

With Ferebe's death in 1623 the connection between Calstone and Cannings was broken. Thomas did not succeed to the living, and even if the people felt affection for George, they would naturally rejoice to have a rector of their own instead of sharing one with 'they girt stups' over the hill.

But 'they girt stups' in their turn could retort that Calstone never entertained the King and Queen of England.

NEIGHBOURS IN THE PEWSEY VALE

After Devizes the most accessible places to Bishops Cannings were the villages in the Pewsey Vale, through which the small road rises and falls gently under the northern rampart of the downs.

At All Cannings Hugh Gough continued for another twenty-five years. Perhaps he went there as a widower who married again; perhaps he only married for the first time. At any rate he fathered five children in the next six years.

He and George Ferebe must certainly have met one another from time to time for, apart from the difference in age, they had much in common. Each served a fine church and a large and scattered parish. Each numbered members of the Ernle family among their parishioners.

In the snug little village of Stanton St Bernard, a mile or so eastwards, sat William Cromwell as vicar early in the century, to be followed for a long spell by Robert Stevens. Writing of Thomas Ferebe's time his son, Nathaniel, told how as a boy he watched a strange clergyman enter the church and approach the altar, set then in the middle of the church. On it a village boy sat idly kicking his heels, but at sight of the visitor he slipped off and stood behind. When the priest, to his surprise, bowed three times, the boy, wishing to be polite, returned the bows.[9] The influence of Archbishop Laud had not reached Stanton.

Further east, but still only five miles from Bishops Cannings boundary, were the twin villages of Alton Barnes and Alton Priors, with churches but a stone's throw from each other yet with different incumbents.

In Alton Priors, in the meadows beside a tributary of the Avon, lived a rumbustious gentleman named William Button, descendant of at least three others of the name.[10] The tall chimneys and ancient brickwork of his home still form part of the old Priory House. In the church a small engraved brass, work of some rude forerunner of Blake, shows his father rising naked from his tomb, while he gazes up at an angel who has wakened him through a long trumpet.

'This was but one, though takinge roome for three,' runs the epitaph :

> Religion, Wisdome, Hospitalitie.
> But since heav's gate to enter by is strait
> His fleshes burde have he left to wait
> Till ye last trupe ope ye wide gate
> To give it entrance to ye soule its mate.

This William Button was the last patron of the little ruined chapel at Beckhampton. His son, squire in George Ferebe's time, may also have been religious—according to his lights. Hospitable, too, though often with other people's venison. His servants, it appears, were in the habit of poaching regularly on the Earl of Hertford's lands, and of bringing the deer to their master.[11] As for wisdom, he showed none, nor Christian charity either in the following episode.[12]

One Sunday he came out from morning service and saw his children with their spaniels and greyhounds hunting ducks on a pond between his house and the church. This must have been the pool, large and clear when I first remember it but now overgrown, where the Avon tributary rose with delicious bubbling and heaving from its sandy bottom. Suddenly a mastiff belonging to a villager named Andrew Dollyn ran to the pond. The idea of the dog of a common man presuming to mix with his own was too much for Sir William, and he straightway set his dogs on the mastiff. The mastiff shook them off and returned to his master in the churchyard. The implacable Sir William followed urging

his spaniels and greyhounds to continue the attack, now reinforced by another mastiff belonging to one of Button's tenants.
Dollyn, seeing his dog getting the worst of it, rescued him, whereupon the hot-tempered and arrogant squire 'did forcibly with a
great staff strike, beat, and grievously wound him and did break
his head so that the blood ran down in great abundance'. 'Con-
ceiving that by the said chance I might be obnoxious to him, I
gave him satisfaction'—no doubt by payment of a coin or two.

But Dollyn, the blood pouring down his head, was definitely
not satisfied, and brought an action against Sir William in the
Star Chamber—unfortunately we do not know with what result.
Incidentally, one of the children playing by the pond that Sunday
would have been the fourth Sir William Button, friend of John
Aubrey.[13]

From Wilcot, the next parish east of Alton, comes a strange
story of bells and sorcery. In the last year of George Ferebe's life,
or possibly during Thomas Ferebe's first year as his successor, the
vicar of Wilcot, William Palmer, who also loved bells, was sum-
moned to his door late at night by 'a debauched personage' belonging to the parish. He wanted, he said, to ring a peal and demanded the keys of the church. Probably, according to a not un-
common custom of the day, he had, after some hard drinking,
wagered his friends that he would do so. But the vicar stoutly
refused. He pointed out that the hour was late, and that the Squire,
Sir George Wroughton, who lived close to the church, would be
disturbed. Thereupon the 'debauched personage' went away in a
rage, threatening vengeance. He was still nursing his grievance
when he met in Devizes William Cantelow, a noted wizard and
astrologer.[14]

'Now here,' thought he, 'is a fellow who can help me'—and
he told him the story of the spoil-sport, Mr. Palmer.

'Ah!' replied the wizard, 'Mr. Palmer of Wilcot. He is said to
love bell ringing himself. Well, he shall have enough of it. That
I promise you.' And from that time onwards one of the bells
sounded continuously in Wilcot vicarage, though audible nowhere else. Cantelow, who confessed that he had brought this
about, was shut up in Fisherton Gaol, Salisbury, nominally for
the rest of his life. Probably other sorceries had been laid to his
charge at the same time. 'The bell will continue to ring as long as

I live,' he declared, a little rashly perhaps, considering how many of his profession were put to death in those days. But Cantelow remained in prison, and the bell continued to toll. People came from far and near to enquire into this extraordinary phenomenon, and caused the Squire great inconvenience, since they always expected him to entertain them. Among the visitors arrived one day a special envoy from King James himself, but neither he nor anybody else could unravel the mystery.

When the King died the Act under which Cantelow was imprisoned was repealed, and probably he was released. At all events peace was restored to the vicarage and the bell silenced at last.

This odd story was told by the Squire's son, Francis Wroughton, who lived to be ninety, to a man named John Beaumont. Francis said that he himself was away at school when Cantelow bewitched the bell, but his father and all the neighbours swore that the story was true. Beaumont re-told it in a curious little book written some eighty years after the event. In his preface he claims to treat his subject 'historically, physiologically, and theologically'. When I first heard of this bewitching of one of the Wilcot bells it fascinated and puzzled me. Since then I have read Beaumont's Treatise for myself and find the story less hard to understand. For the author's ear opened readily to mysterious sounds, and supernatural bells seem to have been his speciality.[15]

No doubt old Francis Wroughton and William Palmer drew on very early memories to make a good tale of a drunken and hot-tempered midnight visitor, and of a wizard's juggling in the belfry. But it also seems probable that Mr Beaumont himself added quite a bit to the story from his own peculiar experiences.

NOTES TO CHAPTER IX

[1] Sir T. Phillipps, *Wilts Institutions*.
[2] In an air photograph taken by the late Alexander Keiller. *W.A.M.* XLIII.
[3] & [4] *Q.S.G.R.*, ed. B. H. Cunnington, p. 16.
[5] Information from Mrs. Sterry, widow of a dew-pond maker.
[6] Quoted by the Earl of Kerry. *W.A.M.* XLIII.
[7] Several times occur the words 'maskells at Michelmas'. Lord Kerry suggests that either the word denotes a Michaelmas tax, or that it meant the right to horse-fodder (marescalia).

[8] The Ducketts owned other estates at Calstone, Blacklands, Cherhill, Stockley, Quemerford and Corsham. Lionel's great uncle, another Lionel and a Lord Mayor of London, bought Calstone Manor from the Zouch family in 1579, and it remained in Duckett hands for close on 200 years. He disinherited his son for marrying the daughter of a servant against 'his express commandment', and in consequence his nephew Stephen succeeded to the estate. The Lionel of Ferebe's time was Stephen's son. He died in 1609 and was succeeded by his brother John—the Duckett who is said to have escaped through the Roundhead forces in a hearse. Pinhills was burnt to the ground, but the Manor at Calstone escaped. Information about the Ducketts comes from *Ducketiana* by Sir G. F. Duckett.

[9] Wilts Tracts. 241. *W.A.M.* Library.

[10] The family claimed to have farmed at Alton since the thirteenth century.

[11] In a petition to James I Lord Hertford declared that 'several men of Alton and Axford . . . being armed with swords, daggers and long piked staves, guns, crossbars, longbows and arrows, and having certain buck-staves and other engines, and divers sorts of hunting dogs as well as grey-hounds and bloodhounds on various occasions entered his parks at Totten-ham, Savernake, and Brimslade'.

[12] This story appears in Star Chamber Proceedings 8/54/11 (Plaintiff: Ralph Baily).

[13] On 'the morrow after Twelfth Night' the two, together with Charles Seymour of Marlborough, attended a meet of the hounds at the Grey Wethers—'One might fancy it to have been the scene where the Giants fought with great stones against the gods,' says Aubrey, describing his day's experiences. Sir William, as a staunch royalist, had already been fined £2,000 for delinquency, so that at this time he was living in his humbler house at Shaw. Yet, though the meet took place only a little over a fortnight before Charles' execution, Button was not too downcast to hunt all day and enjoy a good dinner at Kennet in the evening.

[14] Waylen, *History of Devizes*; and John Beaumont, *A Treatise of Spirits, Apparitions, Witchcraft, and Other Magical Practices* (1705).
William Cantelow, Waylen thinks, may be identified as the owner of the initials in a large elaborate painted horoscope bearing, below a pair of clasped hands, the inscription: 'The nativity of Robert Danvers, Eliza-beth Danvers and their children. By W. C. Done as endorsed, when (they?) were prisoners at Carisbrook.' (Aubrey MSS. The Bodleian).

[15] 'Now as for hearing sounds of bells,' he writes, 'I have never heard of any person who has had so much experience in that kind as myself. . . . In two spiritual visitations . . . some years distant the one from the other . . . I have heard bells for several weeks together, and that of all sorts, from the greatest church bells, to a little Hawk bell (i.e. Priest's bell). Sometimes I have heard a bell gently tolling, sometimes bells ringing solemnly as for a Funeral; sometimes merry round ringing as at weddings. For some weeks together every night as soon as I was in bed a Spirit came with a little bell ringing in my ear. . . . I have heard every night for some time hundreds of spirits coming as it seemed to me, first at a great distance, singing and ringing hand-bells, who gradually approached my house . . . till at length they came to my chamber windows, and some would even come into my chamber.'

PART TWO

CHAPTER X

Queen Anne at Shepherds' Shore

A YEAR after George Ferebe, the mercer's son, was born at Cirencester, a princess, destined to bring much happy excitement into his life was born in a sumptuously furnished castle on the coast of Jutland. Her father, the King of Denmark and Norway, was the richest prince in North Europe, her mother a studious scientifically-minded woman. When the Princess Anne was only fifteen, King James VI of Scotland, who had been undecided whether or not to offer his hand in marriage, fell in love with a miniature of her and decided to make her his wife.

At about the same time that Ferebe set out for Oxford, Anne, married by proxy, started on a far more hazardous journey to join the husband whom she had never seen. Wild storms (raised by witches, or so thought the Admiral who escorted her) began almost at once. Twice she caught a glimpse of her future home and twice the little ship was driven back to the Norwegian coast. Finally, she and her company were forced to take shelter in the tiny, primitive village of Upsloe (Oslo).

An appeal to James to rescue her brought him, in spite of autumn gales, to her side as fast as ship could carry him.

'I am resolvit,' he cried when he read her delicate handwriting, 'to have one romance in my life.' As the old ballad has it:

> Be it wind, be it weet, be it hail, be it sleet,
> Our ship must sail the foam,
> The King's daughter of Norraway,
> Tis we must fetch her hame.

After two re-marriages the royal pair were finally tossed into Scotland by a succession of storms, which cost several hundred old women their lives.[1]

Nor did the young Queen find much peace in that disturbed and intrigue-ridden country. Small wonder if after ten difficult years she said goodbye for ever to a people who seemed to her un-friendly and puritanical—she who put amusement before every-thing. For she inherited nothing of her mother's serious mind. On that progress to England in the wake of James her expectations of a gayer, easier life began at once to be realized. People flocked to pay her homage. Lady Anne Clifford, destined to be one of her firmest friends, and to accompany her to Bishops Cannings, wrote in her diary, 'My mother and I went on a journey to overtake her and kild three horses that day with extreamitie of heate.'

At Althorpe Park, on a June evening, the Queen took part in the first of those masques that continually delighted her. Here, too, she met another woman who became her life-long friend and a companion on her Cannings visit—the beautiful and witty Countess of Derby. From that time onwards movement and enter-tainment grew ever more essential to Anne. Masque succeeded masque. Turn the pages of Nicholls' 'Royal Progresses' and you will be bewildered and dazzled by details of the performances at Whitehall and Hampton Court.

In the country it was the same story. Wherever the Queen went —and she travelled widely about the southern counties—there were always people eager to arrange for her amusement. Her first journey after her coronation was into Wiltshire to stay with the Earl of Pembroke at Wilton, soon followed by a second visit, pro-longed because of an outbreak of plague in London.

Dancing was another of her passions. She had been noted as a child for her nimbleness, and she continued to enjoy it till her final illness. Of her character we get glimpses in the letters of the Venetian and French Ambassadors. The former writes of her as 'affable' and 'of a lively humour, rather good-looking and still more gracious', particularly to those who 'fall in with her humour'. But, on the other hand, 'she is terrible, proud, and intolerable to-wards those she dislikes'. Arthur Wilson says that she was 'a good woman, not tempted to embroil herself . . . content in her own house with such recreations as might not make time tedious to her'. These last words provide the key to her character—her frivolity. And she was terribly extravagant. The sums she spent on clothes and jewels were colossal even for those days.

TROUBLE COMES

Thus Queen Anne's life moved on merrily, and—apart from minor differences with the King, and a growing inability to live on her income—smoothly. But in the autumn of 1612, nine years after her arrival in England, troubles came. The first was a small one, soon remedied. She hated the idea of the Count Palatine, whom she thought insignificant both in looks and status, marrying her beautiful young daughter Elizabeth. Most coldly and 'with a fixed countenance' did she receive him.[2] But Prince Henry, pride of her heart, tall, handsome, athletic, gay, yet at seventeen already impatient of injustice or folly, dragged himself to Whitehall to welcome his future brother-in-law though his own fatal illness was just beginning. Within three weeks he was dead of typhoid, in spite of desperate efforts by his doctors and many strange remedies. His last words were a cry, not for his mother, but for 'my dear sister'. Anne had kept away for fear of infection, her anxiety deepened by a lunar rainbow that hung above his lodging. Now, the desperate struggle for his life over, she was overcome by grief. Miserably she sat in a darkened room at Denmark House uncomforted by her husband, who seldom now lived with her. A tendency to petulance increased. Disparaging remarks burst out about James, about Elizabeth, and little stammering Charles. Depression deepened. But gradually her natural buoyancy came to her aid. Dislike for the Count Palatine lessened and she even showed him some of the affection she had heaped on Henry. For a time she was borne along on the stream of celebrations that preceded the wedding—on St Valentine's Day, 1613—fitting date for a bride destined to be known as 'The Queen of Hearts'.

But when Anne had said a final goodbye to her only daughter— a truly final one, since she never saw her again—depression gripped her once more. Her doctors, seriously worried, urged her to carry out a long-cherished plan to drink the waters at Bath.

And so it came about that on a morning towards the end of April she set out with a large retinue on the journey that was to cause such excited anticipation, such earnest preparation, such crowning delight, in a remote Wiltshire village. The King accompanied her as far as Hampton Court. Then westwards to Windsor, where the first night was spent, rolled the long line of coaches; great square leather-covered coaches that swung to and fro on their poles, and made the term 'to be coached' synonymous with violent motion.[3]

THE COMPANY

What of the Queen's company? That indefatigable correspondent and 'Paul's Walker',[4] Mr. John Chamberlaine, in one of his chatty letters to Sir Ralph Winwood (Ambassador to The Hague) gives us the names of the more important people who travelled with her, and contrasts her retinue with the two ladies-in-waiting allotted to the Princess Elizabeth when she set out on a far longer journey.

'I marvel,' he writes, 'that the Lady Elizabeth went away so meanly attended. . . . The Queen is gone to Bath in great state, for besides the Lord Chancellor, the Countess of Derby and the Countess of Dorset, she hath divers other ladies that follow her; as also the Earl of Worcester, the Lord Danvers, with other noblemen.' He adds, 'Though she made account to stay at the Bath about ten days it is said this journey will stand the King or her £30,000.'

The Lord Chancellor, Sir Thomas Egerton, was a reliable, solid man, an excellent make-weight for the Queen's levity and possibly a curber of extravagance. Far harder jobs had fallen to him, including his struggle to prevent his ward marrying the poet Donne, and his custody of the Earl of Essex. His wife, Alice, Countess of Derby, had won Anne's heart on the journey from Scotland. Her liveliness, her grace, her friendship with poets, marked her out as a fitting companion on a holiday notable for the variety of its entertainments.

The Countess of Dorset likewise met the Queen on her way to England, when she was the care-free thirteen-year-old Anne Clifford, already keeping her famous diary. But now her marriage to a selfish and extravagant husband and the loss of her lawful lands to her uncle had sobered and saddened her. In any case she could never have brought the same high spirits, the same sparkle, as Countess Alice. But she was a well-read, intelligent young woman, and a first-rate conversationalist who, according to John Donne, was capable of engaging the Queen on any subject from 'predestination to slea silk'.

As they drove along this spring morning the Countess's large prominent eyes would note the pleasant, wooded country beside the Thames with no great admiration, nor would she succumb to the charm of the great houses where they were to sleep. For always she longed to be back in her own wild northern lands. It is a pity that, with her powers of observation and her ready pen, she left no record of this particular journey.

The Earl of Worcester, now aged seventy, a tremendous old warrior of the chivalric type, Master of the Horse to both Elizabeth and James, makes an amusing foil to the literary young Countess. Nicholls describes him as 'one of the most complete gentlemen of his time'. He was the earliest of all Anne's English acquaintances, for he it was who carried the congratulations of Queen Elizabeth to James and herself when they landed in Scotland in 1590. Though he had led a hard, adventurous life, the Earl took pride in acting as patron to a band of players. Probably he and the Lord Chancellor and his wife were in the Queen's own coach. We know that he rode beside her through Bristol.

Lord Danby. In the fourth member of the company named by John Chamberlaine we may take special interest, for he was a Wiltshireman returning to the county of his birth and a possible schoolmate of George Ferebe's at Cirencester Grammar School. Furthermore he was a brother of Sir John Dauntsey who rented land in Bishops Cannings. This was Henry Danby, Lord (later Earl) Danvers, born at Dauntsey Manor.

His life, like that of the old Earl of Worcester, was full of adventure. He acted as page to Sir Phillip Sydney and was knighted by Henry of Navarre for gallantry. Aubrey describes him as a man 'of magnificent and munifical spirit', who 'spent £3,000 a year on his kitchen alone and gave and endowed that noble

Physic garden at Oxford'. A portrait by Vandyk in the National
Portrait Gallery shows him with small pointed beard, keen
resolute eyes, and the air of a man who, without arrogance, yet
makes no mistake as to his own importance.[5]

Among the less famous people who accompanied the Queen,
yet more essential perhaps to her comfort, was Lady Drummond,
who came with her from Scotland, had been governess to the
royal children, was, now first Lady of the Bedchamber, and
always exercised a strong influence over her.

There was also the devoted Anne Kroas who sailed with her
from Denmark, attended her everywhere, and stood beside her
as she died. From Denmark, too, Anne brought her own doctor,
Schoverus, and it is highly likely that he, with at least one other,
attended her to Bath.

The little company here described make up the more notable
part of Anne's retinue. That it could only have formed a small
part of the whole we know from detailed accounts of other royal
journeys.

CAVERSHAM

In the early afternoon of April 27th,[6] at their home high on the
wooded hills above the Thames at Caversham, Lord Knollys,
Comptroller of the Household, and his wife awaited the arrival
of their royal guest with an anxious eye on the weather. For it
had rained that morning, and a huge length of crimson broad-
cloth had been laid along the path that the Queen would take.
When the bells of St Mary's suddenly pealed from Reading town
(at a cost of 6s. 8d. for each ringer, according to the church
registers) Lord Knollys knew that soon the Queen's coach would
cross the Thames and climb up the hill. An entertainment in her
honour was ready, down to the last green-clad page, the last
hidden trumpeter. For the Comptroller had acted as host to Queen
Elizabeth twelve years before[7] and well knew what was expected
of him. Thomas Campion had written 'a gallant masque' for the
present occasion, and a troup of young nobles, including the
Countess of Dorset's husband, were waiting to take part in it.
The fun began as Anne and her party approached the park gates.
A Cynic, 'his disordered hair stuck carelessly with flowers', pro-

tests his desire to live in solitude, is converted by an eloquent Traveller, and hastens with him and two Keepers, dressed in 'green perpetuana' to meet the Queen. Trumpets sound among the trees. Hidden voices sing a welcome:

> Welcome, oh welcome, ever honoured Queene,
> To this most blessed place,
> That grove, that tower, that house is happy
> Which you vouchsafe to grace.

At the garden gate a Gardener wearing 'a great pair of slops . . . and a strawne hat piebaldly dressed with flowers', and his Boy 'in a pretty suit of flowerie stuffe', likewise burst into song:

> Paradise were meeter farre
> To entertain so bright a star,—
> But, why errs my folly so?
> Paradise is where you are,
> Heaven above and heaven below.

And so it goes on till, a little exhausted, Anne sups in private with the King's fiddlers playing her 'the solemnest music'. Then the entertainment begins again in the great hall. Lighted by tapers carried by eight green pages she 'adorns the place with her personal dance'.

The next afternoon, enriched by costly presents, she said good-bye to her hosts. But I think that before she left Caversham Lord Knollys got in a few words about George Ferebe. We know from *Life's Farewell* that he continued to take an interest in him after he left Oxford. So, with full knowledge of the Queen's route, he may well have seized the opportunity to show his protegé yet another favour. Would Her Majesty graciously consent to stop at Shepherd's Shore on her return journey and give the clever, musical vicar of Bishops Cannings a chance to entertain her? Her Majesty *did* consent, and we can assume that Lord Knollys sent word to George Ferebe by special messenger. Aubrey says that he received 'timely notice'.

The next night may have been spent at Shaw, near Newbury, home of Sir Thomas Dolman, wealthy clothier and dispenser of

hospitality to many notable travellers.[8] Afterwards Marlborough
was the most usual stopping place, followed possibly by a night
at Bromham Hall, palatial home of Sir Edward Baynton, and
another at Corsham. I think she was entertained at Devizes on
her way.[9]

BATH AND BRISTOL

On the eve of May Day the royal party entered Bath, and under
her doctor's orders the Queen lost no time in taking the waters.
Unfortunately while bathing in the King's Bath she was terrified
by a strange apparition. 'A flame of fire like a candle . . . spread
into a large circle on top of the water,' we are told. Always a
great believer in portents, she considered it 'a supernatural
message from the world below, and nothing would induce her to
enter that bath again'.[10] Henceforth she insisted on using the New
Bath, expressly built for the poor, who never regained their inheritance. After five weeks, her health and spirits much improved,
she moved to Bristol on Friday, June 4th. Here a more lively re-
ception awaited her. Nicholls gives a full account of it. John
Chamberlaine writes on June 10th: 'At Bristow and thereabouts
she hath been entertained with such variety of Delights and
Country Sports that she hath taken great pleasure in the Journey.'
The Lord Mayor, Sheriff, and Aldermen met her at the East Gate
with an oration, and, more welcome, a purse containing over
£100 in gold. Then the Mayor escorted her to the Marquis of.
Winchester's house, and a day or two later entertained some of
her company to dinner, when Lady Drummond presented him
with a diamond ring from the Queen.

On Sunday Anne drove in state to a service at the Cathedral,
with the Earl of Worcester and the Bishop of Wells beside her.
On the following day, the British Navy once more routed the
Turks on the river Severn. The Queen had watched them perform
the same deed on the Thames during her daughter's wedding celebrations. But now she was in more responsive mood. Depression
had completely left her, and she exclaimed: 'I never knew anything so neatly, so artificially performed!' Altogether such was
the enthusiasm of the thousands who poured into the city from
the remotest villages that when she left on June 8th she declared

with tears in her eyes, that she 'never knew she was a Queen till she came to Bristol'.[11]

After a night at Sutton Court, home of Sir Henry Billingsley, she set out on her return journey to London, intent, according to Chamberlain, on 'making more of such progresses'.

PREPARATIONS IN BISHOPS CANNINGS

By early May news had reached George Ferebe of the Queen's return journey from Bath along the old coaching road and of her promise to stop at Shepherd's Shore. From that moment onwards he would be constantly busy, with only one important break in his preparations—a visitation by the Archbishop himself at Devizes on May 31st.[12]

First there were the words and music of his song to be written, and 'the lesson or two' on wind instruments referred to by Anthony Wood.[13] For his singers he drew on his 'scholars', probably the young men and boys in the church choir. Even though Aubrey's claim that Bishops Cannings could 'challenge all England for music' may be an exaggerated one, there must have been good cause for it. True, George Ferebe himself refers to the 'harsh voices, un-tun'd notes' of his singers, and no doubt he still found it difficult not to contrast them with Magdalen choristers. And of course the climate of his time would have made him depreciate any performance before the Queen of England. But, whatever his material, we are told that he taught his chosen band to sing his song 'very perfectly'.

England was a musical land in those days. 'Songs and airs were composed all over the country by persons in every walk of life,' says Trevelyan, and Ferebe's effort would have caused no great surprise. As for the wind instruments, a variety of them would be in common use in Bishops Cannings. Singers and musicians alike must have rehearsed throughout May and early June, and Mrs Ferebe and other women would be busy assembling the 'shepherds' weeds' in which Ferebe had decided to dress his choir. Each man and boy needed a 'pelt coat' of sheepskin and 'clod shoes'—if he did not already possess them. Ferebe had decided to appear as an Ancient Bard. It is interesting to speculate why. Perhaps he wanted to differentiate himself completely from the rest of the company, or perhaps he felt that 'Lobcock fashions' (as he calls their dress) involving a generous display of bare legs, would not be becoming to his forty years.

When Aubrey later put forward his theory that Stonehenge was a Druid Temple he was only giving shape to old rumours and tales. Ferebe's Bard no doubt belonged to this Celtic tradition and demanded a flowing white robe and beard. Thus attired he would assume the character, not of a Druid, but of one of their innocent cousins, an English counterpart of the French 'Bardi', who Camden says, 'to the tune of the Harpe sang ditties in verse, containing the famous exploits of brave and noble men'.[14] And in addition to all the singing practice Ferebe would expect his ringers to practise harder than ever they had done since the bells were first hung. Luckily the hay harvest would scarcely have started, so both singers and ringers could count on a fair amount of leisure.

By Wednesday, June 9th, when the Queen and her company turned their faces towards London we can picture the village humming with excitement. Last touches were being added to costumes; last experiments made with ruddle so that legs, arms and faces should appear properly reddened by 'Boreas' rough, tempestuous blasts'; last rehearsals taking place in the Parsonage garden, watched by any who chose to peep through from Chandler's Lane or to loiter in the churchyard. From such vantage points they would see the troup of men and boys—in all likelihood at least sixteen of them, since the music was composed for four parts—singing the ten verses of their song with appropriate actions, while Ferebe beat time and the sound of their voices floated round the village. Everything must go without a hitch on the great day and there was certainly a final rehearsal at Shepherd's Shore. Here the company must practise just when and how to climb out of Wansdyke and group themselves before the Queen.

THE JOURNEY TO SHEPHERD'S SHORE

When Anne left Siston her next two nights, to judge from other royal precedents, were spent either at Lacock Abbey, or perhaps the first at Corsham and the second at Lacock.

The journey that lay ahead of her on June 11th was not one to be taken in a hurry. In spite of numerous Highway Acts practically all roads remained deplorable by modern standards. Deep ruts abounded, filled either with water, mud, or suffocating dust. But there were degrees of badness. Once the royal coaches had crossed the Avon and climbed Bowden Hill they could continue In comparative ease along the outskirts of Pewsham Forest.[15]

Following the line of the Roman Road they would come by Sandy Lane and the probable site of the old buried city of Verlucio near Wan's house. So far so good. But in front lay a far more formidable bit of country the like of which the Queen perhaps had not travelled since she came from Scotland. But before she and her party reached it, and after they had turned off the Calne road, they would stop at the famous inn, The Brown Bear— later just 'The Bear'—for refreshment and a change of horses, which Sir Edward Baynton perhaps supplied. The tall mellow brick house with mullioned windows still stands, though much enlarged, restored, and no longer an inn. Close by is a smaller, humbler place then called The Bell, now a farm house, where, in the pleasant little wainscotted parlour, the coachman and servants of travellers were entertained. The Queen's head coachman, however, before flinging off his red cloak and accepting food and drink, would be sure to enquire about the state of the road ahead, whether or not a counterpart of the royal 'way-wiser' of Elizabeth's time had already sent in his report. Even on a fine day in June Bagdon was no joke for the drivers. Forty years later a coachman was killed as he urged his horses up the steepest part.

About 1700 a rather tiresomely facetious and vulgar fellow called Ned Ward (who nevertheless is worth reading for the glimpses he gives of the country through which he travels) writes of this part of his journey in his 'A Step to the Bath', 'The road was so rocky, unlevel and narrow . . . that I am persuaded the Alpes are to be passed with less danger. We jolted so cussedly that I thought it would make a dislocation of my bones.' Walk the old road for yourself, and you will realize what lay ahead of the royal party. It starts with deceptive gentleness as a wide grassy track, but before you have gone half a mile you will be amazed to think that even a light cart, let alone cumbersome coaches, could have mounted it. Narrower and narrower it grows

and the gradient sharpens with every step. Though the tunnel of
thorns and hazels through which you pass would not have been
there when the road was in full use, you feel no doubts about its
uncompromising nature as, sunk deep in the chalk, it rises to a
height of 700 feet. In wet weather, when it changes to a milk-
white river, journeys up Bagdon Hill must have been appalling.

Small wonder then if the Queen's coachman failed to feel completely relaxed as he sat in the Bell parlour. As for the royal party,
it is anyone's guess what they ate at The Brown Bear. Perhaps the
famous 'Sandy Lane Pudding'[16] had not yet appeared there; but
probably some at all events enjoyed the cider praised by Ned
Ward. In any case it is unlikely they stayed long, for Anne would
not forget that somewhere in the outlandish bit of country ahead
Lord Knollys' country parson awaits her with his village players.
So the long line of coaches takes to the road again. On their left
they pass 'Weekefield',[17] where a little later Aubrey tells us
'houses and coales for at least a quarter of a mile long and a great
quantity of Roman money', were discovered; also an earthen pot
full of money which his servant stole from him.[18]

Now they reach Hell Lake—or 'Hillock'—deep in mud at most
seasons because of a small stream that rises there, though doubt-
less on this particular day full only of dust and ruts. An old milestone pokes up through the undergrowth, but it belongs to the
later half of the century. Further on is Hitchin Lane where teams
of oxen assembled in bad weather to be harnessed to the coaches
before they climbed the last and worst bit of the hill.[19] Nearby on
the right another track turned south for Nether Street and Devizes;
part of its course is still easily traceable. The old road itself grows
very lovely just here, and the banks on a June day are gay with
rock-roses, milkwort, shepherd's thyme, and small butterfly
orchises. South of it the downs are excitingly carved and grooved
so that seen from below they resemble a line of small volcanoes.
Fold after fold they end at last in the lonely magnificence of
Oliver's Camp, known in Anne's day as Bromham Castle.

Could she, leaning through the window of her coach to watch
the striving, sweating horses, have looked instead into the future
she would have seen, galloping down this same road and down the
precipitous hillside on her right, a crowd of desperate, beaten men
—many to meet their deaths when their horses stumbled and fell,

and to be buried in Bloody Ditch at the foot of the hill or in neighbouring churchyards. Though it would have comforted her to know that these men were flying from her son's army and that her grandson, Prince Maurice, was among its leaders, another and longer look into the future would have shown her how brief and barren was the royal victory.

The top of Bagdon is reached at last. The exhausted horses are given a short breathing space. The coachmen's hearts lighten now that this dangerous lap of the journey is over. Ahead lies comparatively level country, with Roundway Down stretching away to the right, and Kings Play Down rising steeply above the little hidden village of Heddington. The road widens once more and another milestone pokes up through the grass. Had it existed then the coachmen would scarcely have believed that they had driven only one mile since they left The Brown Bear. The royal party had at last entered the parish of Bishops Cannings.

AT SHEPHERD'S SHORE

George Ferebe, knowing well that the Queen could not stay long in his parish, would lay his plans carefully, and since the curve of the hill made on-coming travellers invisible at Shepherd's Shore a mounted messenger probably kept watch from 'Vuzz Knowle'. Standing on top of it he would see the line of coaches as they drew near to 'Calneway'. Another messenger must have been ready to gallop to the village to warn the ringers, assembled ready in the belfry. One of them was no doubt posted on the roof outside awaiting a signal. When it came the eight bells would be swinging lustily within a few minutes, sending their voices to the top of the downs.

Meanwhile, as the procession wound under the hill and the first passenger galloped back to the shore with news of its approach, excitement must have reached fever point. Ferebe, in his flowing white robe, would be giving last emphatic directions before someone fixed a beard of sheep's wool on his face and adjusted his wreath. His singers were packed in the bottom of Wansdyke and the parish constables would keep the rest of the crowd in place. Since royalty cast almost as big a spell then as now, it can be taken for granted that most able-bodied men and women in the parish—from Horton and Coate and Roundway as well as from Bishops Cannings, Bourton and Easton—had come up on foot, or in rough carts or mounted on horse or donkey, to share in the fun. Here would be gathered all the Cannings families whose names have endured into the present century together with scores of others. Every child old enough would be there, including Elizabeth Ferebe and her two brothers (aged seven and five), the little Slops from Westend and Easton, innumerable Ruddles, the curate's four children, the schoolmaster's Susannahs. Many of the shepherds, too, who kept their sheep on surrounding hills—on Rough Ridge, on Morgan's Hill, on Roundway, Beckhampton, and Calstone Downs—would either have left their flocks or have driven them within convenient distance of the 'Shard'. For was not this an entertainment that paid them special honour?

As for the place itself, in some ways it looked much as it does today. Here was Wansdyke dropping from Tan Hill and sweeping up to join the Roman road. Here were ancient burial mounds. Here, though scarcely the same, a few little hardy trees—ash, oak and thorn—to offer shelter and shade. But the Shore would have worn a more civilized, lived-in air. For here stood the little inn already spoken of, the benches for the shepherds, the smooth well-cropped pastures of Shepherds Bench Lawns and the Breach Lands. Though no sheep feed there today countless flocks have grazed on them in the past.

All round the Shore, 700 feet above the sea, stretch the same 'wild, wide, houseless downs' celebrated in Ferebe's song, only far wilder when he wrote the words. For of late years the plough has crept higher and higher, and one or two houses have appeared. But still this is untamed country, especially when autumn and winter storms rush over it. As has been seen men have perished here from the cold, and here a young shepherd was found dead, face downwards, because there was no one at hand to help him when he fell in a fainting fit. But now it was high summer and the throng of people, including the shepherds who knew the worst of Cannings down, were all in summer mood. Every eye would turn westwards as suddenly round the bend of the hill the carriages rumbled into sight and drew to a standstill.

Then out stepped Ferebe in his long white robe and bowed low to the foremost coach. Assisted by the important gentlemen who

accompanied her, the Lord Chancellor on her right and the Earl
of Worcester on her left, Anne descended from her carriage, and
Ferebe spoke the little rhyme that he had made for the occasion,
which Cannings folk have loved to repeat ever since:

> Stand still, great Queen, amidst your loving people,
> And listen to the bells of Bishops Cannings steeple.[20]

In the silence that fell the sound of those bells would be clearly
audible.

Pressing as near as they dared, staring over each other's
shoulders, the crowd saw a woman with the gleaming golden hair
that some of them knew by repute, though it no longer hung
'seemly down her princely shoulders' as at her coronation, but,
much be-frizzed, was piled high on her head. They saw a comely,
plumpish woman who looked good-humouredly at them from
lively brown eyes. Her dress would be all that could be expected
of a Queen, since she had a passion for sumptuous clothes and
travelled with a fine disregard for rough, cross-country roads. If
she wore a cloak it was thrown aside before she left her coach.
There was the great farthingale from which she never parted,
that grew larger and larger as she grew older, in spite of James's
loathing for it; the bodice cut low to display her famous snow-
white skin; the upstanding lace collar behind her head. Nor would
jewels be wanting to dazzle country eyes. She possessed an immense store and felt naked without them.

Not till the onlookers had taken in every detail would they
spare a look at the Queen's companions and discuss their identity.
John Ernle probably knew Henry Danvers already. It might well
be that Sir John Danvers, who later farmed a considerable portion
of land in the parish, had ridden across the downs from Dauntsey, both to do honour to the Queen and to meet his brother. If
so the eyes of the women would rivet themselves on him, for we
know from Aubrey that he was so strikingly handsome and 'his
complexion so beautiful, that during travels abroad people would
crowd after him in admiration'.[21] But his character hardly
matched his looks. 'He was a proud, formal, weak man,' wrote
Lord Clarendon.

What did the Queen in her turn see as she stared in friendly fashion at the assembled crowd? First of all, of course, George Ferebe, proud, happy, a little absurd in his rig-out. It may be that his wife stood beside him, in a full-skirted dress but no farthingale, or perhaps, as a simple village woman she chose to withdraw a little into the background. No doubt the two churchwardens, Daniel Elson and Thomas Neate, and the curate, were close by. And here, too, would be Thomas Cook, the Bishop of Salisbury's land agent, and all the more important of Ferebe's parishioners. Of these, Sir John Ernle, even if he had to ride up from Whetham instead of from Bourton, would certainly be one, bringing with him his wife and family. It is an interesting and justifiable specu-lation that among them was a boy to whom indirectly Aubrey owed his knowledge of the events at Shepherd's Shore. This was John, elder of Sir John's twin sons. As has been seen he became father to the Sir John Ernle who was Chancellor of the Exchequer to James II and an intimate acquaintance of Aubrey's. What more likely than that this seventeen-year-old boy retained a lively memory of the scene, described it to *his* son, and handed on to him a copy of 'The Shepherds' Song'? This son, in his turn, re-peated the story to his antiquarian friend, who was always on the look-out for an interesting tale, and allowed him to make a copy of the words.[22]

Sir John—I refer now to the squire of Ferebe's day—ranked with his wife, Margaret, heiress of the Haydocks of Blunsdon, as county folk, and would naturally be more fashionably dressed than other country gentlemen, such as Robert Nicholas of Coate, Griffin Nicholas of Roundway, and Simon Unwin of Horton. Lady Ernle, their daughter, Frances Ernle (about to marry Thomas Mylma) and Sir John's step-mother, Lady Susan Reynolds, perhaps sported farthingales, though not such huge ones as the Queen's. Far more numerous, however, than the gentry were yeoman farmers like Thomas Slop of Easton and George Ruddle of Five-acres, and all the humbler tenants of the Manor—the yeomen in doublets of leather or broadcloth, the small tillers of the soil in fustian tunics (Puck's 'hempen homespun') wide loose breeches, and coarse woollen stockings or canvas leggings.

But more important than anyone else was the band of singers and musicians who, dressed in their 'shepherds' weeds', waited in the bottom of the Dyke for a signal. Then, 'drawing up to her,

they played a most admirable lesson on the wind instruments',
which, being done, they sang 'their lesson with four parts with
double voices'[23] beginning :

> Shine, oh thou sacred Shepherd-starre
> On silly shepherd swaines,
> Greeting with joy thy shepherdesse
> Along these champion plaines.

This song was naturally the highlight of the entertainment.
Though Ferebe refers to 'Rhymes composed so lightly' (and
certainly there is nothing in it that could have cost him much
labour) and though Aubrey believed the music to have been considerably better than the words, a pleasing country honesty
breaks through the artifice in places. The metre is the old 'four-
teener' of Sternhold and Hopkins' Psalms, and the music (of which
I have been unable to trace a copy) would have been in the nature
of a hymn tune.

At any rate Aubrey tells us that The Shepherds' Song was 'by
Her Highnesse not only graciously received and approv'd, but
also bounteously rewarded, and by the right honourable, worshipful'—that is by the Lord Chancellor, the two earls, and the two
countesses—'and the rest of the general beholders warmly
applauded'. Indeed, it would need a very dry-hearted queen and
tough attendants not to be pleased with the simple, earnest efforts
of this village troop, standing in the midst of their proper surroundings, the Wiltshire downs, blowing their pipes and singing
their sweetest. Anne was no carping, peevish Queen to exclaim
like Hypolyta, 'This is the silliest stuff that ever I heard!'—even
though in the minds of herself and her two friends, Countess
Anne and Countess Alice, may have risen an involuntary comparison with their own magnificent dresses and the exotic settings
of previous masques. Instead of sky-blue taffeta and cloth of
silver here were only 'country swads' in skin coats and homespun
gowns; instead of a background of jewelled glass, downland
flowers in June abundance. Instead of cherubs spouting water
from their mouths, the song of larks.

But the Countess of Derby at least, with her ready wit and wide
sympathies, must have delighted in the contrast.

Ferebe refers in his song to a rumour that the Queen, watching other country pastorals, has made innocent fun of them. No matter, he says. Let her laugh, yet be pleased at the same time.

Some two months later Anne was entertained by an elaborate procession arranged by the tradesmen of Wells, which included 'a cart of old virgines . . . their attire made of cowtayles, and bracelets of harnes . . . hanged about their necks',[24] (presented by the butchers and tanners). Though Ferebe refers to the way in which rough winds and winter frosts have changed his young men (with their ruddled faces) into 'these ugly formes', they certainly looked beautiful compared to this strange cartload.

Not only was the Queen genuinely pleased with her Cannings entertainment but we are told by Wood that ever after she valued George Ferebe for his ingenuity. The 'bountiful reward' of which Aubrey speaks was presumably the Chaplainship-in-Ordinary which the King bestowed on him.[25] Moreover, Ferebe's song was not something 'graciously received' only during its performance. For the author, intent on making the most of his opportunity, had sent it off beforehand to be printed in London, and within a few days was able to send a copy 'within a compartment excellently well engraved and designed with goates, pipes, sheep-hooks and corucopias'—all the romantic equipment of a shepherd in fact—to the Queen.[26] Her attendants also received copies, since Wood remarks elsewhere[27] that the words of the song were printed and dispersed about the Court. The musical part of the entertainment over, George Ferebe stepped forward again with an Epilogue—'to the great liking and content of the Queen and her company'. But nothing more than that is known of it.

By this time it must have been fully three in the afternoon. A journey over roughish country lay before the royal party, even if, as is probable, they got no further than Marlborough that night. The coaches roll away over the downs towards Beckhampton, while up at Shepherds' Shore George Ferebe and his company stand watching till they are out of sight:

> Yet as thou goest, our Prayers our loves
> Our heartes, shall follow thee.

The crowd gradually disperses, some to their homes, some to

[23] Anthony Wood (*Fasti*). He gives only the first two lines of the song. For the entire song see Appendix at end of book.

[24] Brit. Arch. Report, 1860.

[25] Anthony Wood speaks of it in connection with the visit of Queen Anne, and Aubrey when he writes of James I coming to the parish five years later. Enquiries from various sources have brought no further evidence about the conferring of this distinction.

[26] The following entry occurs in the Stationers' Registers (Vol. III, p. 240) for June 16, 1613: 'Mister Dight. Entered for his copy under the hands of Master Nyd and Master Harrison, Warden, a thinge called 'The Shepherds' Song' before Queen Anne in 4 parts completely musicall upon the playnes of Salisbury.' Incidentally it may have been these last words that led Miss Strickland to place the proceedings in a 'wild ravine' on Salisbury Plain. Perhaps Mr Dight, ignorant of Wilts geography, put it 'upon the playnes of Salisbury' on his own initiative, as sounding more exciting than plain 'Shepherds' Shore'.

[27] Wood, MS. 19.D (4) 52. (Bodleian) 'Biographical Notes on Musicals.'

CHAPTER XI

King James at Coate Field

AN exceptionally cruel winter gripped England the year after Anne's visit. In one parish register the snowfall is recorded as 'the greatest which ever fell upon the earth within man's memorie . . . Passengers both horse and foot passed over gates, hedges and walls . . . to the great fear and admiration of all the land, for it came from the four parts of the world, in the south as well as in the north, and continued daily increasing until the twelfth day of March, upon which day (being the Lord's Day) it began to decrease'.[1]

But even on May Day morning it still lay so thick that 'instead of fetching flowers, the youths brought in flakes of snow'. The Cannings shepherds had a heavy task trying to save their sheep as continuous snowstorms swept from the downs into the village and deep drifts lay everywhere. Death took his toll, too, among the villagers. Seven died within six days, among them a young son of Thomas Sloper of Easton. The big church must have been bitterly cold on Sundays, and Thomas Nash and Arthur Sloper, the churchwardens, would turn a lenient eye on empty pews.

A drought which lasted most of the summer followed this desperate winter and spring, and brought fresh hardships to the tillers of the soil.

When James announced his intention of making one of his costly visits into Wiltshire that summer, a petition begging to be excused the honour was sent to him. The signatories pleaded the suffering and privations in the county due to the frost and the drought 'whereby cattle are exceeding poor and like to perish everywhere'. The petition remained unheeded. James travelled when and where it pleased him.

Meanwhile the seasons came and went in Bishops Cannings

with their gifts and their penances, while the village grew slowly and George Ferebe's own reputation increased.

Then, in 1618, five years after the Queen stopped at Shepherds' Shore, exciting news once more reached him. The parish was to be honoured by another royal visit—this time from the King. Anne, entering on her final illness, was not to accompany him. Even had she been well enough it is unlikely that she would have come, for Buckingham's ascendency was increasing and the royal pair spent less and less time together.

George Ferebe's fertile imagination grew busy again. This time not only should there be singing and ringing, but the organ must peal out and a game of football played to amuse a depressed king.

We can only guess why James decided to make a public appearance in Cannings. Perhaps he wanted to meet, if he had not already done so, his 'Chaplain in Ordinary', the Wiltshire parson who had so pleased his wife and her friends. Perhaps Lord Knollys had been busy again on his protégé's behalf. 1618 was a memorable year for many reasons. With true English interest in the weather Camden finds time to record how towards the end of January it was 'like summer; in so much that flowers in the garden and fields appeared, and thrushes hatch their young birds to the astonishment of all men'. But while primroses and celandines burst into bloom and birds were busy in the hedgerows there was no answering spring in James' heart. He suffered increasingly from arthritis and gout, and also from ever mounting debts. Even worse was the news from abroad affecting both his daughter Elizabeth and the whole Protestant cause. Yet, to the indignation of his people, he could not make up his mind to send help because of his over-riding desire to please Spain—Spain who flattered and deceived him the whole time. So he decided to cut himself free for a while from the tangle of foreign affairs and the mutterings and grumblings about him, and to visit once again the pleasant land of Wiltshire.

First he would spend a few days with young Sir Edward Baynton at Bromham Hall, at the foot of the downs and close to forests full of deer, where he had stayed at least twice before. After that he would meet George Ferebe and his parishioners at Coate Field before he proceeded to Salisbury to create still more knights and barons. He made no less than 700 about this time, and among

those thus honoured on this Wiltshire visit was George Wroughton, the Wilcot squire who was so plagued five years later by
visitors seeking information about the bewitched church bell.

But James had no intention of spending his whole time in
adding to his Exchequer. He would sweeten business with a few
days' hunting in Cranbourne Chase from the Earl of Salisbury's
house.

It seems likely that he left London about the 26th July, three
days before his fifty-second birthday, when the bells of St
Margaret's, Westminster, rang a peal in his honour. With him
went his usual large and costly retinue. But Sir Thomas Egerton
was not of the company. In March the King, with tears in his
eyes, for he genuinely loved him, had received back his Seal of
Office. The faithful old Chancellor felt too ill and weak to serve
him any more.

Probably the royal party travelled by Shepherds' Shore and
Bagdon Hill—the directest way to Bromham Hall, which stood at
Netherstreet only a short distance from the old coaching road.
It was a magnificent house, built round three sides of a quadrangle,
'fit to entertain a king, and nearly as large as Whitehall,' people
said. His host, a young man of twenty-five, educated at Christ-
church, and M.P. for Devizes when only twenty-one, was rich,
influential, and owner of much land. In Bishops Cannings he held
a considerable piece of the downs with pasture for 1,000 sheep,
as well as meadow land round Lay Woods. He would certainly
do all in his power to please the King and give him the chance to
shoot a dear.

So next morning off went James into the woodland, presumably
on horseback and riding in the extremely awkward fashion of his
later years. No longer, perhaps, did he wear the dress 'green as
the grass he trod on', described satirically by a contemporary
writer. Beside the water in Lackham Park he shot a stag near
enough to the Avon for a horn to be thrown into the water. Thereupon the owner of Lackham claimed the deer for himself in
accordance with an ancient custom. 'On my soul,' said James
good-humouredly, 'he was a wise King who made such a grant.'[2]

Since not so many exact dates are available as for Queen Anne's
progress in 1613, the order of events here given is partly guess-
work. But we do know that it was on Saturday, August 1st, that

the King, while staying with Baynton, made Rawlyn Bussey of 'Bruncham' a knight.[3] Probably this ceremony took place early in the day, and James then passed through Devizes on his way to Coate Field. Though the bells of St Mary's pealed it is doubtful whether Devizes townspeople were feeling particularly warmly towards him. The broadcloth industry in Wiltshire had suffered disastrously through his personal interference with the 'Merchant Adventurers', and though its privileges had been restored in 1617 'the damage had been done and the whole cloth trade thrown out of gear.'[4] Among the small weavers existed much suffering and unemployment, which was destined to grow steadily worse with the start of the Thirty Years' War. Moreover, as he drove by, some of the burgesses would watch him with slightly jaundiced eyes as they muttered together of the expenses that all these visits incurred.[5]

From Devizes the royal party made its way to Coate Field, probably by the Marlborough road and then along the small one that turns off beside the Barracks. After half a mile along it they would reach a spot now known as Clay Hole, where, I think, the inn referred to by Aubrey as 'The Bush' must have stood. Above it and left of it stretched the wide piece of pasture land called Coate Field,[6] and another road leading to Etchilhampton ran in from the south.

Here the King was met by George Ferebe and his parishioners, who included a party of singers dressed in carters' frocks and carrying whips. At the right moment they burst into the four-part 'bucolics' that their vicar had written for them. Unfortunately this time Aubrey left no copy behind him. James, much troubled by rheumatism in his knees, no doubt remained part of the time seated in his coach. The crowd, pressing round for a glimpse of him, were not rewarded by anything in the least glamorous. They saw a man who, only fifty-two, was yet ageing fast, with few teeth in his head and an unruly tongue that refused to stay in its proper place. Since he suffered from constant catarrh he was forever sneezing and blowing his nose, and he had a habit of rolling his eyes 'in a most unpleasing way when he looked on strange people or objects'[7]—including, perhaps, the Cannings carters cracking their whips and opening wide their mouths. Yet George Ferebe at least would see in this ungainly figure the man who in spite of all his follies, his absurdity, his pedantry, truly loved the Church—the man to whose influence he partly owed the beautiful version of the Bible that he read aloud every Sunday. With Ferebe would be the two churchwardens for the period—men who were a part and parcel of Bishops Cannings —John Ruddle and William Sloper. Though half a dozen of each of their families had died since the coming of Queen Anne, these had been replaced by a fresh battalion of young Ruddles and young Slops.

With her three step-children Mrs. Ferebe once again watched a triumph for her husband, and once more all the important people in the parish gathered to welcome a royal visitor. Nicholases from Devizes, from Roundway, from Coate—all very handy to The Bush—would be here, as well as Robert Drew from Southbroom and Simon Unwin from Horton. Edward Ernle had only a mile to come from Etchilhampton Manor, and even if no Ernles occupied Bourton just then, John, so closely knit to Bishops Cannings, would surely have ridden once more over the downs from Whetham.

And once again I think it was his eldest son who gave Aubrey the story of the King's entertainment at Coate Field.[8] Anthony Wood is out of it this time. Perhaps as the years slipped by news of men who, like Ferebe, had been lost to Oxford for nearly twenty years, became increasingly hard to garner. And Wood had no such local sources of supply as Aubrey.

As the singing ceased the sound of the Cannings bells, travelling over the flat meadowlands, once again reached royal ears. The organist, too, 'playing for state' made his instrument thunder its loudest. Perhaps, in his enthusiasm, he managed to delude himself into thinking that the King would hear it a mile away.

After the bucolics came the football, a game which James had himself opposed in earlier years, as 'meeter for the laming than the making able'. Now he evidently accepted it as a part of English village life. How the young men of Bishops Cannings today would smile had they been spectators! Instead of thirty players in jerseys and shorts each keeping to his appointed task, here was a rabble dressed in heavy country clothes, tumbling each other all over the place, unhampered by boundary lines, unworried by umpires. For football was a wild undisciplined recreation in 1618. The few rules varied in different localities to suit the ground, which was often of the roughest.[9] Coate Field might be uneven but far less so than many of the places where the village boys were in the habit of practising. Their ball was a pig's bladder blown out 'great and thin'.[10]

But however absurd the match played before the King that August afternoon might seem to modern eyes, it would be remarkably vigorous, lively, and skilful in its own way. Bishops Cannings, it must be remembered, was already noted for its football.

But the game could not have lasted long since James faced a journey of nearly twenty miles across the Plain that same day. He would take the southern road over the hill till he struck the old Lydeway; then on to Red Horn Hill, travelling possibly by the very same route as the great sarsen stones some 2,000 years before. Probably as he passed Stonehenge he stopped for another look at the mysterious circle that had fascinated him at an earlier date.

The next morning—a Sunday—he was creating with elaborate ceremony two new Earls in the Great Hall of the Bishop's Palace, adding thereby £40,000 to his Exchequer. Nearby, in his dingy lodging, poor broken Sir Walter Raleigh, covered in sores,[11] sat writing his hopeless apology for the disastrous voyage to Guiana.

At Bishops Cannings George Ferebe would surely in his sermon make some gay and eloquent reference to the happenings at Coate Field. Probably several of his congregation were still a little bruised and sore from the game of football.

NOTES TO CHAPTER XI

[1] C. Cox, *The Parish Registers of England.*
[2] Waylen, *History of Devizes.*
[3] Nicholls, *Royal Progresses.*
[4] Ramsey, *The Wilts Woollen Industry.*
[5] The Devizes Chamberlains' Accounts. On this occasion 2s. was given to William Helies 'for his paynes in looking to such goods as were sent to Bromham'; £22 was paid to the King as a forced loan; there were sundry expenses in cleaning up the town beforehand, and 20s. 8d. for 'repairing the Causewayes'. During a visit in 1613 fees to the King's officers alone came to £20 15s.

⁶ Its position is shown in the Tithe Award map of 1819. It was from the upper part of this big field that Waller bombarded Devizes.

⁷ H. A. Wilson, *James I of England*.

⁸ For Aubrey's account see Appendix C.

⁹ Stubbs, in his *Anatomie of Abuses*, called it a 'bloody and murderous practice where everyone lay in wait for his adversary, seeking to overthrow him and pick him on his nose, though it be upon hard stones'.

¹⁰ G. M. Trevelyan, *England under the Stuarts*. Many magistrates also tried to suppress the game early in the century because it drew men away from archery practice.

¹¹ John Chamberlain.

PART THREE

CHAPTER XII

The Last Days of George Ferebe and the Coming of Thomas Ferebe

DURING the November after James' entertainment at Coate Field 'a mighty blazing comet' filled innumerable hearts with fear and anxiety for the future. At Hampton Court Anne, a firm believer in omens, and slowly dying of dropsy, eyed forebodingly 'the stupendous harbinger'. Arthur Wilson definitely connected it with her death. 'The Common People,' he writes, '. . . thought this great light in heaven was sent as a flambeau to her funeral'.[1]

And while the comet flamed in the sky, Anne Kroas, her faithful Danish maid, held a candle in front of the Queen to lighten the final darkness.[2]

James survived his wife by seven unhappy years. His health worsened, his early popularity waned, his policies grew more and more ill-advised. Among other foolish deeds he clapped John Pym, member for Calne, and perhaps the most able of the Parliamentarians, into prison. Distress due to the start of the Thirty Years' War was rife everywhere. The weavers of Devizes and its neighbourhood suffered increasingly and had little money to spend.

Many people in Bishops Cannings must have felt the pinch. Market days in the little town were soberer than they used to be, bargaining harder, the meeting of friends and neighbours less light-hearted.

But where church life was concerned the coming of John Davenant to Salisbury brought new hope and inspiration. His goodness, his learning, his gentleness, his passionate desire for unity as opposed to uniformity, impressed his opponents as much as his own followers and made him a favourite with the King. In the twenty years of his episcopate he did much to restore the spiritual life of his diocese.[3]

But George Ferebe only lived to see the beginning of his work. Two years after Davenant's consecration he died at the age of fifty. The cause of his death is unknown, but we may guess that it was sudden because he had made no will—an unusual omission in those days.

John Barnston, a Canon of Salisbury, 'Comissary to the worshipful the dean and chapter of Salisbury Cathedral' took charge of his affairs and appointed 'Elizabeth Ferebee, spinster, natural and true daughter of the said deceased' to be sole executrix.[4] That Ferebe's wife, Bridget, was passed over in favour of his daughter seems to show either that she could not read or write, or that she was considered unsuitable, because she was not the children's own mother. Elizabeth, aged twenty-two, was chosen as the only one who had come of age. Her elder brother, Thomas, was eighteen and the younger Thomas fifteen. Since the registers contain no further reference to George's wife or children they presumably left the parish after his death.

Among the signatories to the deed of administration was Arthur Sloper, churchwarden at the time and father of the last baby whom George Ferebe baptized. George's brother John journeyed from Poole Keynes and Thomas from Woodchester to add their names and to attend the funeral, which took place on Michelmas Day, 1623. As it was a holiday and harvest over, most of the villagers would flock to show their respect—and, I think, their love—for the man who for thirty years had tended them, prayed with them, preached to them, taught them to sing, and added much colour and fun to their hard lives.

George was buried under the long, twilit chancel. This we know because, though no memorial tablet survives, Thomas asked in his Will to be laid beside him there if he himself should die at Bishops Cannings. When the deep voice of the tenor bell boomed across the meadows and the downlands, the men who were tending sheep round Shepherds' Shore must have remembered the June day ten years before when their parson had cried out:

'Stand still, great Queen, amidst your loving people
And listen to the bells of Bishops Cannings steeple.'

No such happy, care-free days would dawn again for a long while.

Thomas Ferebe

John Ferebe, second son of Thomas the mercer, had acquired the Cannings living from the Ernles,[5] and on George's death he presented it to Thomas, youngest of the three clerical brothers.

After he left Magdalen in 1606 Thomas was appointed by Sir George Huntley[6] to the living of Woodchester, beautifully set on a wooded hillside near Stroud in the heart of the cloth-making country. His church, standing close beside the home of his patron, has perished, but the old churchyard, full of ancient and interesting tombstones, remains, and below its surface lies a portion of fine Roman pavement, undiscovered in those days. Though the wool trade flourished exceedingly when Thomas first went to Woodchester,[7] unemployment was causing great distress[8] the year before he left, and he must have felt glad to move to a more prosperous village. John himself took on Woodchester in addition to his other parish of Poole Keynes.

With Thomas came his wife, Martha, and their two children—Elizabeth, aged eleven, and George, aged nine. Martha died in 1630, and in 1632 he returned to his old neighbourhood for a second wife, Ann Essington, whom he married in Coaley church. Elmcote Farm, where she lived, still stands.[9]

Life throughout George Ferebe's time, in spite of hardships, had been comparatively peaceful and uncomplicated. But, during the years that followed his death, Thomas and all the clearer-eyed of his parishioners would notice a slow darkening of the horizon. When the shepherds dropped at evening from the serenity of their downs their wives brought rumours from Devizes market of trouble in London and elsewhere, till at last they themselves heard the roar of guns on Roundway, watched groups of flying horsemen pursuing each other over the wide grasslands, found dying soldiers,[10] and on one occasion at least had their sheep stolen, as when 644 of Sir Edward Baynton's flock were carried off to Oxford by the Royalists.

In the village the people groaned over the maraudings of the

army and the exactions heaped on them by the rival bands who
straggled off the inhospitable downs demanding food. The village
constable's life was made a nightmare by orders constantly pouring in first from one side and then another. If he pleaded that they
were impossible of fulfilment it was at 'utmost peril both to his
person and estate'. Michael Paradice, a constable in an outlying
part of the parish, was left dead on Wick Green by a party of the
King's horsemen because he was unable to satisfy the authorities.
Other constables and tythingmen prayed for release from their
arduous duties. One complains of 'his great prejudice and losse
by reason of these troublesome and distracted tymes', and
another begs to be relieved of his 'tythingmanshippe'. When we
read some of the orders which they were expected to enforce we
understand their misery. One day the Cannings constable must
send a party of men 'such as are of able bodies . . . mechanics,
tradesmen or others rather than husbandmen' to 'the Devizes'
to work for the Royalists. On another the Parliamentarians required all the able-bodied in the tithing to come armed with
'spades, shovels, pickaxes and other tools', to 'throw down all
such fortifications as are now standing about the Devizes'. Again,
200 'able and sufficient men' must appear by break of day to
work for a week in building up the 'bull-works at the castle' on
behalf of the King. The Royalists urgently demand 'three score
pounds' from Bishops Cannings and Potterne, while in the same
year the Governor of Malmesbury exacts no less than £240 from
them for the upkeep of the Parliament's dragoons.

Not only must the parish furnish money and men but it must
share with Potterne in sending '40 loads of good and sufficient
hay' to the Castle. No longer could Cannings farmers count on
taking their cheese and butter and corn to market; they might at
any time be required to deliver large quantities to one army or
the other.

Nor did the sufferings of the villagers end with maraudings by
soldiers and exactions by the authorities. In 1646 an outbreak of
plague spread a blight over their lives. While they were still paying for the relief of victims in Devizes, 'the said infection came
into divers houses' within their own parish and £20 was needed
for local help—'and all this' they say in their petition, when
many people in the parish are 'disabled by being so much

plundered when the Rowte was' (or, as a correction 'the business on Roundway Hill'), 'that they are not able to relieve their owne poore'.[11] In the year of 'the Rowte' conditions were so bad that the Quarter Sessions at Easter and in July could not be held.

Thus during his twenty-seven years at Bishops Cannings Thomas Ferebe watched dissention grow in Church and State, and during his last decade he must often have been deeply troubled both by the sufferings of his people and by the problem of his own allegiance in these bewildering days.

From Woodchester sad news reached him of the indignities and hardship inflicted on his brother John by the Parliament troops; of how a soldier tore his surplice from him and mockingly wore it himself; of how they stripped him of his clothes, leaving him only a pair of drawers, and marched him bare-footed to Gloucester. When old friends in Cirencester sent money by a kinsman serving in the Parliamentary army for his ransome, the man kept it for himself, and John remained for some days confined 'in a damp low room under the College school without a fire.'[12]

In 1642 'a worthy and learned gentleman' named Thomas Chadlicot made a vigorous effort at Bishops Cannings to reconcile King and Parliament in a speech delivered in the presence of 'one Master Blithe, a Minister of God's word, and Master Lewin, a Councillor of Law'.[13]

Chadlicot's oration started off : 'Gentlemen, this Kingdom is about to hasten on the road-way to ruin . . . to be brought to such a miserable existence that it cannot be capable of a greater misery. It is now the mock and bye-word of foreign nations; it is become an enemy to itself, and goes about to daub its lippes with the blood of its own children.' He enlarges on the horrors of Civil War, and advises 'the plucking from their places of refuge of such Malignant and Diabolical persons . . . as have made a discord betwixt the King and Parliament . . . which, being done, by God's providence, the King's goodness, and Parliament's industry . . . this may be made a most happy and flourishing kingdom.' It is interesting to think of this earnest and eloquent appeal going out from a remote Wiltshire village.

Thomas Ferebe evidently was unwilling to associate himself with a man who sought the downfall of Archbishop Laud. He never became a Conformer, but he did receive an 'augmentation' of his living amounting to £16 for the half-year ending September, 1649, from the Sale of Dean and Chapter Lands.[14]

But though his own peace and that of his parish was constantly disturbed during his later years, any picture that suggested continual unrest and dis--ease between George's death and his own would be false. For nearly twenty years life went on pretty much as usual. Slopers and Ruddles, Merritts, Nashes, Neates, Wiltshires, Minetys, Stevens and many another old Cannings family, continued to cultivate their land, to marry and bear babies. The population rose from about 350 in George Ferebe's time to over 460 while Thomas was vicar.

The Manor Courts continued to meet, to issue orders about boundaries and the cleansing of ditches, to fine those who overstocked Cannings Cow-downe or broke the pinfold.

As for Thomas' domestic life, four sons and two daughters were born to him and Anne between 1633-43. His eldest daughter, Elizabeth, child of his first wife and baptized at Woodchester, was married in St Mary's Church in the summer of 1635 to a Chippenham gentleman named Henry Bull.

Thomas made his Will in February 1651,[15] when he describes himself as 'an unworthy preacher of the word of God' but declares himself 'of Perfect minde and memory'. He was, however, nearing seventy, and by June of the same year he was dead.

In addition to other bequests to his seven children (his eldest son George had pre-deceased him) which were to be paid by their mother out of her estate when they came of age, he left them presents of a number of eleven shilling pieces that would be found lying in 'a little painted box'.

Owing to the wretched state in which Archdeacon Macdonald later found the registers for that particular period no burials are recorded for a whole year between March, 1651, and March, 1652. So, though his death is unrecorded, there is every reason to believe that Thomas was laid in the grave of his elder brother according to his own wish.

After forty-eight years there was no longer a Ferebe at Bishops Cannings Vicarage. Nor apparently did any of Thomas' family remain in the village. The most likely guess is that some of them moved to Chippenham to join Elizabeth Bull, because Mary (or Maria) the youngest daughter, also took a husband belonging to the town. Her married life was short; she died in childbirth when only twenty-six. On her monument in the church her father is referred to as 'Thomas Fereby, de Episcopi Cannings, nuper vicarii dignissimi'. Thomas' youngest son Henry, too, is spoken of as belonging to Chippenham when he married an Essington cousin. Ann herself and her other children probably returned to her old district, and it may well be that the 'Thomas Ferrbee, yeoman', whose death is recorded in Frocester parish register in 1654, was her second son—the one who as a small boy scribbled his name on the Carrell at Cannings.[16]

Thomas Ferebe, the vicar, was succeeded by Thomas Etwall, member of another prolific Cannings family. After the long un-settled period of the Civil War he, like so many, found his home in a sad state of repair, and it is he who tells us in the registers that he had his roof re-laid and that he built himself a new kitchen and added chimneys. Thus strengthened and improved the old vicarage, standing so close to the church, beseiged continually by the sound of bells, continued to house his successors for close on another 200 years.

NOTES TO CHAPTER XII

[1] Arthur Wilson, *Life and Reign of James I*.

[2] Strickland, *Lives of the Queens of England*.

[3] Morris Fuller, *Life of Bishop Davenant*

[4] 'Letters Commissary' at Somerset House. 'Natural' at that time meant true-born or legitimate. Its present use was not widespread till at least 100 years later.

[5] Sir T. Phillipps, *Wilts Institutions*.

[6] Sir George Huntley was buried by Thomas in 1622. A fine canopied tomb that once stood in the old church, and was moved to the new one is generally considered to be that of himself, his wife, and family.

[7] *Men and Armour in Gloucestershire* shows that of 61 men at this period in Woodchester 35 were engaged in the woollen industry. Towards the end of Thomas Ferebe's time there unemployment grew steadily and there was much distress.

[8] For information about Woodchester I am indebted to extracts from a History of Woodchester by Mr Little, published in the Woodchester Quarterly Pamphlet in 1919, kindly sent me by H. A. Randall, whose wife is a descendant of the Gloucestershire Ferebes.

[9] Elmcote, in the parish of Coaley (usually 'Cowley' in those days) was called Hulmancote in the seventeenth century. In the eighteenth century it became Helmcote. c.f. 'A Rough draught and measurement of Mr

Nathaniel Underwood's land late Essingtons, in Coaley.' (No. 7961. Glos. Collections. Glos. City Library.) See also map of Helmcote Farm. No. 7943. I am indebted to the Rev J. Aubrey, vicar of Coaley, for information about Elmcote. Later the Essingtons lived at Gossington Hall. (*Vide* Glos. Visitation, 1682.) The family seem originally to have been London merchants. Two of Anne's brothers were such, and her eldest married the daughter of another.

[10] *Vide* the Registers of Bishops Cannings and other villages under the downs.

[11] For this and other details of exactions see Waylen's *History of Devizes*; also Q.S.G.R. for seventeenth century, ed. B. H. Cunnington.

[12] J. Walker, *Sufferings of the Clergy*. For more about John see Appendix 4.

[13] A copy was 'Published for the Public Good and for the Cure of the miserable Distempers of this distracted Kingdom' on Aug. 26, 1642, in London.

[14] See W. A. Shaw, *History of the Church of England during the Civil War, Vol. II*, Appendix VII. In this same volume (p. 548) Shaw gives 'D. Ferebe of Oriel' as 'minister of Bishops Cannings' about 1649, but I have not been able to identify him, nor is there any allusion there or elsewhere to Thomas Ferebe having been superceded. He was vicar of Bishops Cannings when he died.

[15] In Somerset House. P.C.C.

[16] If this was so he died young (very probable, as his name does not appear again) two days after his wife gave birth to a daughter. An Anthony Ferebee succeeded him at Frocester and fathered six children there. He may have been a cousin from Cirencester—a son of George Ferebe's youngest brother Anthony—who took on Thomas' farm after his death.

CHAPTER XIII

Epilogue

M Y story of a Wiltshire village in the seventeenth century is over. It only remains to follow its fortunes briefly up to the present day.

The population continued to increase till it probably realized its peak of 1246 in the mid-nineteenth century. Then the rapid decline that impoverished thousands of other villages throughout England set in, till today there are only about 600 people in the whole parish. During this period many ancient cottages, that nestled round the church or in little sociable groups in the fields, crumbled away or were burnt to the ground and never replaced.

Not only have people and houses dwindled, but the sheep, too, though happily there is still at least one flock. But the immemorial figure of a shepherd with weather-beaten face, cloak and crook, no longer stands on the top of every hill.

Ferebe's wild downs have been greatly tamed. No traveller is now led astray by mysterious music; none gets benighted; no 'poor wandering people' perish from cold and exhaustion. Every ploughing season the combines batter their way higher and higher till at last only a few strongholds, such as Morgan's Hill and Furze-Knoll, resist. All of us who remember the wide uncultivated, unfenced spaces, so springy, so exhilarating to walk on, may perhaps be forgiven our nostalgia even while we are conscious of a new beauty and excitement in the new pattern of activity. Sometimes, if you stand at twilight high on the Roman road or on Easton Hill, instead of the shepherd leading his flock to the fold, you will see great scarlet machines twisting and turning in the fields below you. With their long necks, their beaks, their strange excrescences, they appear grotesque prehistoric monsters wallowing in a green or yellow sea. But at least all the lonely barrows that have escaped demolition, the Roman road itself and the Dyke, the coaching road and Old Shepherds' Shore are, it is to be hoped, safe from their maraudings.

In the mid-eighteenth century an adventurous boy named William Baily, born in 1736, descendant of an early 'Belly', left his father's small holding for the sea. Twice he sailed round the world with Captain Cook. Later, as assistant to the Astronomer Royal, he went out to the North Cape to observe the transit of Venus. When, after his retirement, he visited his native village, he consulted Mr Brown, the churchwarden, how he could best help it. Mr Brown pointed out that the church organ was in a sad state, and William, who had accumulated a comfortable fortune, decided to present a new one. In 1811 it was installed with much musical ceremony. Since Bishops Cannings could not now provide as many musicians as in Ferebe's day, Avebury, six miles away, was called on to help. Special music was written by an Avebury man, and a 'crotchet weaver' from the same village played 'a serpent' that he had made himself. Before he died in 1880, aged 97, the old man described the occasion to Thomas Kemm of Avebury Manor.

Not only did William give an organ but also an endowment fund. Today, after a recent renovation, it is still in use and Cannings children delight to look up and read about the voyage with Captain Cook.

I have spoken of how Bishops Cannings slowly changed after George Ferebe's time till its old reputation was largely lost and forgotten, and it became a butt for surrounding villages. But late in the eighteenth century the shepherds who kept their flocks round Wansdyke made a brave and funny effort to emulate their forefathers. People scoffed at them as simple, did they? Well, they would show that they too could entertain royalty. For someone had told them that George III was to pass through the parish on his way back to Windsor—almost certainly along the new highroad, since by this time (1789) Bagdon Hill was in exceedingly bad repair and little used. So the shepherds erected 'an arch of wool' across the road where it cuts through the Dyke at New Shepherds' Shore, and asked His Majesty, 'together with our beloved Queen, Princess, etc.', to pass under it. At the same time they presented him with a copy of some excessively bad verses written for the occasion by a gentleman referred to as Mr C.F. of Roundway. The vicar, Arthur Dodwell, was evidently not an 'ingenious man' like his forerunner. Nobody, it seems, felt equal to reciting the verses, much less singing them.

> Pray stop your worthy Majesties
> And cast your eyes around,
> To view we rustic shepherds,
> And the flocks upon the ground.

So it continues for six stanzas, till it ends:

> And now we all must leave you
> Your journey to pursue.
> We wish you safe at Windsor,
> The Queen and Princess too.[1]

Some 170 years before other shepherds had sung:

> Yet as thou go'st our prayers, our loves,
> Our hearts shall follow thee.

At the end of the eighteenth century an enterprising company started to make the Kennet and Avon Canal. Since some seven miles of its course is in Bishops Cannings the inhabitants felt proud that now, though their village still lay right off the high-road, they had been linked directly with a wider world.

Barges bringing coal from the Mendips, or loads of sand and gravel from the neighbourhood of Bath, passed along, and anyone who took the field path to Horton might see the swing-bridge open to let them through, might watch the unharnessing of the horses, and exchange repartee with the bargees. Sometimes great tree trunks floated by on their way to the wharf at Honey-street, or rafts of hay from the wide grass verges. The landlord of the Bridge Inn, a half mile to the west, carried on a brisk trade in those days.

Not only did the canal bring glimpses of another life, but in winter, when the frost was hard enough to defeat the ice-boat, grown-ups and children slid and skated to their hearts' content.

Pike and eels provided many a dinner, and in its still waters some of us learned to swim. Thus did the canal become a much loved feature of the village, and so remained till rail and road traffic robbed it of its purpose. Today it is usually deserted and weed-bound and no barges pass along it; its ultimate fate hangs in the balance.

In the year of Waterloo a keen and lively young vicar, fitting successor of Ferebe, came to the village, married two wives, fathered ten children and stayed on for forty-seven years. This was Archdeacon Macdonald, who enriched Bishops Cannings with his scholarship and his deep interest in its history and its people. If they were simple he loved them the better for it. He it was who had a new vicarage built in 1863 at the northern end of Parsonage Field, a little further from the clamour of the bells. Scarcely had he settled in than he heard a noise like an express train, and a whirlwind, rushing past the house, tore the slates from his roof. Just 200 years earlier neglect and decay forced Thomas Etwall to relay the tiles of the old vicarage. Now violent weather drove another vicar to repair his brand-new one.

Thirteen years after his death both the fabric of the thirteenth century tower of the church and its foundations were found in a dangerous condition. The bells must ring no more. Extensive restoration must be undertaken at once both inside and out; the tower be braced with iron bands; crumbling stones removed, surfaces re-faced. Somehow a very large sum of money was raised and the work well and truly done. Once more the spire and the little steeple could look down in safety on the village; once more the bells could ring. When the completion was celebrated there had perhaps been no greater event in Bishops Cannings since Bishop Jocelyn started to build some 700 years before.

My father[2] shared George Ferebe's love for bells, and saw to it that the old reputation of the parish was maintained. Often he rang with his men, and incidentally he added one more Cannings tale when, after an evening practice, he stepped one windy night from the belfry on to the leaden roof of the nave to cool himself, heard the door bang behind him and realized that he was shut out in the dark. The ringers had all gone and there was nobody to hear his shouts. But after a while the sexton came through the churchyard and rescued him.

It was under this vicar's leadership that the Cannings team rang their first peal of grandsire triples after many a hard struggle. When he could not take charge himself the schoolmaster or the sexton lent a hand. The sexton would wag his chestnut beard at young recruits, and say, 'You rang your bell as nice as ninepence.' One old man still remembers the words with pride. Sometimes, however, came stalemate.

'Look 'ee!' cried a young man despairingly to the schoolmaster, 'if 'ee do keep a-calling' Bob and nawt but Bob us'll never get no forrader.'

So if the early fame of Bishops Cannings for football and music faded, its ringing prowess remained. But there was a brief unhappy time in the beginning of the present century during which the ringers refused to mount the belfry stairs. It happened like this. Nuts and ale had long been the accompaniment of ringing practice. The deep recesses of the belfry windows used to be as full of broken shells as a squirrel's hoard. Less sightly were the beer bottles. But when the bell-ringing vicar left the parish a temporary curate-in-charge declared that such goings-on could not be tolerated. Furthermore he decided that the men must remain for service after a Sunday peal—a custom many tended to neglect. War was declared. The ringers in a body went on strike, and only the tenor tolled alone on Sundays. The well-meant efforts of a band of amateurs soon met with disaster. One little man hung on to his bell too long and flew skywards. He dropped his sally just before his head hit the ceiling. All the same he had to keep to his bed for a fortnight. Another sprained his thumb. The ringers, lurking among the tombstones, listened with innocent malice to the strange behaviour of first one bell and then another. An old ringer still loves to talk of that time with a mischievous twinkle. At last, after weeks of silence or a sad mess-up among the bells, peace was restored and the old team returned to the belfry. I'm not sure about the beer bottles. I think they gradually ceased to be carried up in overcoat pockets.

In the early seventeenth century it is probable that the ringers seldom rang anywhere but in their own belfrys. But during the latter half of the nineteenth century began the interchange of visits between village teams, that, confined at first to a radius of a few miles on bicycles or in horse-drawn brakes, now cover many counties. Cannings ringers go by specially chartered buses into Gloucestershire, Dorset, Devon, Hants, Berkshire and Oxfordshire. They ring the bells in one church after another, sometimes just a straight peal, sometimes an arduous one of 5,040 changes, and involving four hours without a break. On such occasions a man walks round feeding them from a spoon. Long after darkness has fallen they come driving down to the village, tired but proud. For a long time they talk of their experiences; of how the clapper of one enormous bell fell down with a noise like thunder so that for a moment they thought judgment day had come; of how pleasant to them were the bells of X, and how harsh those at Z. But always they agree that none in all the countryside sound so sweetly as their own.

For over 350 years now a little band of men united by love of their craft have climbed the dark stairs to the belfry, pulled off their coats or jerkins, gripped their sallies, and set their bells tumbling in the twilit heart of the tower.

Many ringers have died in the last few years, and some are growing too old to handle a bell any longer. But, so that there shall be no failure in continuity, a band of children, both girls and boys, including one ten-year-old, are learning to ring. If George Ferebe could rise from his tomb under the chancel, climb the stair and take a peep into the belfry how pleased he would be.

Though it is unlikely that a Queen will ever stand again at Old Shepherds' Shore and listen to village singers I believe that the bells of 'Bishops Cannings steeple' will send their music across the downs for many a generation yet.

NOTES TO CHAPTER XIII

[1] *The County Magazine*, November, 1789. B.M.
[2] Charles Hony; he became vicar in 1874.

APPENDIX A

THE WILL OF THOMAS FEREBE, SEN.

In August, 1611, Thomas Ferebe, confessing himself in August, 1611, to being 'sicke in bodye' though 'praised be God in sound mind and perfect memorye', made his Will, four months before his death. It was perhaps fortunate for his family that he did not postpone it any longer because the fortunes of those who died intestate sometimes fell into the hands of sharks. Such a one, indeed, was the bishop who gave probate for this particular Will —namely Sir John Benet, 'Master, Keeper or Commissary' of the Prerogative Court of Canterbury, who had a weakness for selling an interest in the estates of intestate people to the highest bidder.

To the poor of 'Ciscester' Thomas left forty shillings, and to his wife Elizabeth twenty pounds a year. But it was to Anthony that the bulk of his property went—namely the house in Chipping Street, already referred to, also 'my newe house which I latelie builded in Chippinge Streete, adjoyning to the house aforesaid' and his three houses 'in St Ciceley's Streete'. To John his father bequeathed forty, and to Thomas, thirty pounds on their mother's death, and also granted them remission of their debts. His elder daughter Elizabeth was dead, but his youngest one, Mary, was to have his 'biggest pott and brass pans', and, like her mother, 'a mourning gown of blacke'. To his 'well beloved' brother George, his brother-in-law, John Hopkins, and his son-in-law, Roland Freeman, who were all witnesses of his Will, he gave 5s. 8d. each.

APPENDIX B

DREW'S POND

Drew's Pond was once much beloved by Devizes people. Its origin is uncertain but Waylen suggests that it was the very fishpond ordered by Henry III from the Constable of the Castle for his personal use when he stayed there. Certainly there used to be fine fish in it. To children it was an exciting, romantic spot, with its bulrushes, its wealth of water birds, its bent and ancient trees. In the middle, to crown all, was a small island. 'Oh, for a boat to reach it!' they would think—not guessing that there was a time when Devizes people *did* go boating on the Pond, once with tragic consequences. On a Sunday afternoon in the mid-eighteenth century a young couple and their friends borrowed a beer-cooler from a neighbouring cottage and paddled it into deep water. The beer-cooler, a shallow, awkward vessel, overturned and all five were drowned. Their fate is commemorated on a hideous obelisk in St John's churchyard engraved with the words 'Remember the Sabbath Day, to keep it holy.' Ruth Pearce had blasphemed and fallen dead in the Market Place some fifty years before, and now these wrong-headed young people had broken the fourth Commandment and met their deserts. The Mayor and Corporation could not resist using them as a warning for posterity.

But over half a century later a little boat moved happily about the pond. Musicians played on the island, and tents containing refreshments were set up on the banks. The occasion was a county party given on a summer evening by William Salmon, rich influential Devizes lawyer jokingly known as 'King Salmon', whose house stood close to the pond. It was election time, and he had decided to entertain lavishly on behalf of his own candidate. Among his guests was Tommy Moore from Bromham, who records the party in his Diary. 'Everything,' he wrote, 'was gay and riant.' If plain John Drew had been able to take a peep at

his Pond on this August evening in 1819 he would, according to
George Ferebe's description of him, have called such goings-on
'fantasticall' vanitie'. Only a trace of the famous pond now
remains.

APPENDIX C

THE ROYAL VISITS

EXTRACTS FROM 'FASTI OXONIENSIS'
BY ANTHONY WOOD

'George Ferebe was admitted the same day (July 7, 1595). He was afterwards Minister of Bishops Cannings in Wilts, one of the King's chaplains, and author of *Life's Farewell*, etc. This man, who was a Gloucester man and well skilled in music, did instruct divers young men in his parish in that faculty till they could play or sing their parts. In the year 1613 Queen Anne, the royal consort of King James I, made her abode for some weeks in the city of Bath purposely for the use of the waters there. In which time he composed a song of four parts and instructed his scholars to sing it very perfectly as also to play a lesson or two (which he had composed) on their wind instruments. On the eleventh of June the same year the Queen in her return from Bath did intend to pass over the downs to Wensdyke within the parish of Bishops Cannings: of which, Ferebe having timely notice, he dressed himself in the habit of an old bard and caused his scholars (whom he had instructed) to be clothed in shepherds' weeds.

The Queen, having received notice of these people, she with her retinue, made a stand at Wensdyke; whereupon these musicians, drawing up to her, played a most admirable lesson on the wind instruments, which, being done, they sang their lesson of 4 parts with double voices, the beginning of which was this:

> Shine, O thou sacred shepherds'-starre
> On silly shepherd swains', etc.

which being well performed also, the Bard concluded with the Epilogue, to the great liking and content of the Queen and her company. Afterwards he was sworn Chaplain to his Majesty, and was ever after much valued for his ingenuity.'

FROM JOHN AUBREY'S 'NATURAL HISTORY OF WILTS'

'Mr. Ferraby, the minister of Bishops Cannings, was an ingenious man, and an excellent musician, and made several of his parishioners good musicians, both for vocal and instrumental musick. They sang the Psalms in consort to the organ which Mr. Ferraby procured to be erected.

When James I was in these parts he lay at Sir Edward Baynton's at Bromham. Mr. Ferraby entertained his Majesty at the Bush in Cotefield with buccolics of his own making and composing, of 4 parts; which were sung by his parishioners who wore frocks and whippes like carters. While his Majesty was thus diverted, the eight bells (of which he was the cause) did ring, and the organ was played on for state : and after this musical entertainment he entertained his Majesty with a football match of his own parishioners. The parish in those days would have challenged all England for music, football, and ringing. For this entertainment his Majesty made him one of his chaplains-in-ordinary.

When Queen Anne returned from Bath he made an entertainment for her Majesty on Cannings Down, sc. at Shepherds' Shard, at Wensdyke, with a pastoral performed by himself and his parishioners in shepherds' weeds. A copie of his song was printed with a compartment excellently well engraved and designed with goates, pipes, sheep hooks, cornucopias, etc.'

'THE SHEPHERDS' SONG BEFORE QUEEN ANNE

voy'ct in foure parts and compleatly musical which was by her Highnesse not only graciously received and approved, but also bounteously rewarded, and by the right honourable, worshipful and the rest of the general Hearers and Beholders warmly applauded, in Wiltshire the elventh day of this instant June, the yeare of Our Lord, 1613.'

> Shine O thou sacred Shepherds-starre
> On silly Shepherd swaines
> Greeting with joy thy Shepherdesse
> Along these champion plaines.

What, dost thou stay thy motion here?
And does thy Grace-ship grace us?
This honour we esteem next that
When God in Heaven shall place us.

From fair Aurora's first arise
Till silent night begins
The day-guide Phoebus, with his beames
Doth search our tawny skinnes.

And Boreas rough tempestuous Blasts
With Winter frosts and stormes
Have changed our habit and our hew
into these ugly formes.

How dare we then (like Corydon)
In every part unsightly,
Salute our Empresse all renowned
with rhymes composed so lightly?

Our comfort is thy Greatness knowes
Swarth faces, coarse cloth gownes
Are ornaments that well become
The wide, wild, houseless Downes.

Sometimes Thou look'st on Country Swadds;
(As Fame abroad doth bruite)
And mak'st them objects of thy mirth
(Dear Queen) the same's our suite.

Deal so with us, be pleasd with Clownes'
crabb'd lookes, clod shoes, pelt coates,
Blunt Lob cock-fashions, unbiliev'd,
harsh voices, un-tun'd notes.

O, that the powers Divine would grant
our eies might have their fill!
With greedie gaze insatiate
We would behold thee still.

But Thou must pass, and we must loose
The Sight that now we see,
Yet as Thou go'st, our Prayers, our Loves,
Our hearts, shall follow Thee.

*This song, which has not, as far as I know, been reprinted since
Ferebe published it, I found among the Aubrey M.S.S. at the
Bodleian. Above his copy (hand-written) is a shield ornamented
with a crown and the letters A.R.*

*Writing of the Queen's entertainment (in his chapter on 'Shep-
herds and Pastorals.' Nat. Hist. of Wilts.) Aubrey says: 'A copie
of the verses is here annex'd, but I believe the musicall com-
position was much better.'*

JOHN FEREBE
(with notes on two other Johns)

John Ferebe, baptised in Cirencester Parish Church in June, 1579
—and thus three years younger than George—entered Magdalen
Feb. 4, 1591-92, aged 16 (Alum. Oxon. Foster). He did not take his
B.A. till 1601—from Magdalen Hall—and his M.A. in 1606. He
was ordained in 1603, and in the same year became Rector of
Poole Keynes (called 'E. Pole or Poole' in 'Wilts Institutions')
then in the Salisbury diocese—a small village in the basin of the
upper Thames, with houses of Cotswold stone. It lay in that part
of Wiltshire whose inhabitants Aubrey describes as 'Phlegmatique
. . . slow and dull; heavy of spirit. . . . They feed chiefly on
milke meates, which cools their Brains too much and hurts their
Inventions' (*Nat. Hist. of Wilts*). But John, perhaps because he
was not one of the 'Indigenæ or Aboriginæ' did not so suffer.
After spending the greater part of sixty years at Poole he died,
aged 86, with a mind which had lost none of its vigour, even
though his body was so feeble that he had to be carried into the
pulpit. Words to this effect were inscribed in Latin (so Aubrey
tells us) on a stone that stood in his day in the chancel of Poole
Keynes church, but is now missing. Though John suffered so
grievously at Woodchester, he remained unmolested at Poole,
where the surrounding country was predominantly Royalist. His
own squire, Sir Neville Poole, who fought on the Parliament side
and helped to defend Marlborough, had his house burnt down by
Royalist soldiers. In an eloquent letter he appealed to the Speaker
of the House of Commons for help because of his subsequent
sufferings. (Quoted by Sir R. Luce in his MS.Hist of Malmesbury.
W.A.S. Library, Devizes, Shelf 153.)

John Ferebe had a son and a daughter by his wife Margaret.
Though both were christened at Woodchester in 1625, it is certain
that the son John, at any rate, was born six years earlier else-

where (he is unrecorded at Poole K.) since Foster puts him down as 17 when he entered Oriel in 1636.

The Rev. T. M. Layng, who helped me much in my early inquiries, writes: 'One of the P.K. Rectors consistently baptized his family (immediately on birth) privately at home, and then later repeated it publicly.'

This younger John was curate for a time at Oaksey, close to his father's home, and later became vicar of Ashbury, Berks (formerly in Salisbury diocese). A stone on the chancel floor records that he and his wife died within four days of each other in 1681.

His son Edward lived on in the parish, had two daughters, and was 'buried in woollen' in 1691.

It seems possible that a Michael Ferebe, whose wife Margaret bore him three sons and four daughters, all baptized at Poole Keynes, was another son of John of Ashbury. From *Alumni Oxoniensis* we know that he was the father of the Thomas who matriculated at Magdalen Hall, July 8, 1670.

Yet another John Ferebe, a son of John, brother of Thomas of Cirencester, and a cousin of George Ferebe, was an 'intruder' at Theydon Guernon, Essex, from 1645 till his death in 1652. He was 'an able godly minister', who 'freely and voluntarily set up and for some time constantly and gainelessly maintained, a lecture at Epping'. (T. Davies, *Evangelical Nonconformity in Essex*.) He took the place of Dr. Nicholas Wright, who preached only 'twice or thrice a year, yet got his parishioners into trouble for attending other churches in order to hear sermons'.

APPENDIX E

NOTES ON THE FEREBE FAMILY

The Ferebes, whose name derives from Ferriby on the banks of the Humber, and means 'by the ferry', were at one time widely scattered in eastern counties and in Gloucestershire. In this latter the family—under a large variety of spellings—occurs during the sixteenth, seventeenth and eighteenth centuries in the parish registers of Stroud, Frocester, Uley, Owlpen, Coates, Rolleston, and Minchinhampton, among other places. At Brimscombe they were connected for at least 100 years with the Phoenix Ironworks.

In the old family home there, lived together for some sixty years four sisters who asserted their separate individualities in many funny ways. Their gardener grew, and the cook cooked, four different kinds of potatoes. Each had her own brand of tea, her own cake, her separate plate of bread-and-butter. The last died in 1944, aged 95. They were the descendants (of the fifth generation) of Edward Fereby, a broadweaver of Owlpen, buried there in 1713.

Early in the last century a John Feribee kept the Old Crown on Uley Green, and was clever at increasing his business. An amusing story is told of him in *Glos. Notes and Queries* (Vol. V., p. 195). One dark evening a stranger arrived on horseback and asked how far it was to Owlpen Manor. 'Surely, sir, you don't think of going there on such a night as this,' said old Feribee.

'Indeed I do. Business presses,' replied the stranger. 'Which way must I turn?'

'Why,' was the answer, 'you must go along the Green and down the hill by Fiery Lane till you come to Cuckoo brook, then a little farther on you will pass Horn Knep, after which you will go by Dragon's Den. Next you go through Potlid Green, then by Marling's End and that will bring you straight into Owlpen, but you must take care not to miss the road.'

'If it be so long and troublesome a way,' said the traveller, 'then I think, landlord, if you have a bed I will stay till morning.' So Feribee gained a guest for the night and the traveller saved himself a journey of not more than ten minutes!

Mention has been made of the Ferebes who settled in Frocester in the mid-seventeenth century. It is highly probable that they came from Cirencester and were related to George and Thomas.

In Cirencester the name appears frequently in parish registers and other records. Thomas the Mercer had three brothers living in the town. One of these, George, also in the family business, appears in *Men and Armour in Glos. in 1608* as a man then between 50 and 60. Here also we find Thomas' youngest son Anthony and his servant (and cousin) Edmund. Two copper plates in the church (removed from tombstones) commemorate two Edmunds —one who died in 1628 and another in 1687.

The treble bell, cast in 1722, is inscribed with the name of 'Mr Thomas Ferebie', one of the churchwardens who procured it 'by a subscription'. Ferebes also often occur as Jurymen in the seventeenth century in Cirencester. In 1600 Thomas' brother John signed with eleven others a deed respecting land at Longhope. At Siddington, close to Cirencester, a Mr Charles Ferebee was churchwarden. Of him Southey, in his *The Doctor*, quotes a bill that he owed to Joseph Cook, which ran, 'To mending the Commandments, altering the Belif, and making a new Lord's Prayer, £1 1s. 0d.'

Instances of clerical Ferebes are numerous in Gloucestershire (as also in Essex) though not all remained in the Anglican Church. One became Minister of the Baptist Chapel at Sodbury.

I have only come across one Ferebe who was, like George of Cannings, a rhymster. In *The Orrery Papers*', Vol. I (ed. the Countess of Cork and Orrery) is a letter written by Lord Orrery in 1735 to 'the Rev Mr Ferreby at his house at Westminster', where, after an allusion to Dean Swift as 'that inimitable man whose company he cannot enjoy half enough because of his lawyer's interference, he ends: 'I had almost forgot to thank you for a beautiful copy of verses. . . . You that write so well should write oftener, and pray choose a better subject than Orrery.'

[For much of the information in this appendix I am indebted to H. A. Randall, whose wife is a niece of the old Miss Ferrabees of Brimscombe.]

INDEX

The references to a family in this index include not only references to the family as a whole, but also references to all those members of the family who do not receive a separate entry. Sources of information do not, generally speaking, appear in this index. Names in italics are names of fields. Where there are many references, the most informative are listed first, and are separated from the remainder by a semicolon.